AS/A-LEVEL YEAR 1
STUDENT GUIDE

OCR

Psychology

Component 2
Psychological themes through core studies

Molly Marshall

PHILIP ALLAN FOR
HODDER
EDUCATION
AN HACHETTE UK COMPANY

Philip Allan, an imprint of Hodder Education, an Hachette UK company, Blenheim Court, George Street, Banbury, Oxfordshire OX16 5BH

Orders

Bookpoint Ltd, 130 Milton Park, Abingdon, Oxfordshire OX14 4SB

tel: 01235 827827

fax: 01235 400401

e-mail: education@bookpoint.co.uk

Lines are open 9.00 a.m.–5.00 p.m., Monday to Saturday, with a 24-hour message answering service. You can also order through the Hodder Education website: www.hoddereducation.co.uk

© Molly Marshall 2015

ISBN 978-1-4718-4418-8

First printed 2015

Impression number 5 4 3 2 1

Year 2019 2018 2017 2016 2015

This Guide has been written specifically to support students preparing for the OCR AS and A-level Psychology examinations. The content has been neither approved nor endorsed by OCR and remains the sole responsibility of the author.

Typeset by Integra Software Services Pvt. Ltd., Pondicherry, India

Cover photo: agsandrew/Fotolia

Printed in Italy

Hachette UK's policy is to use papers that are natural, renewable and recyclable products and made from wood grown in sustainable forests. The logging and manufacturing processes are expected to conform to the environmental regulations of the country of origin.

Contents

Content Guidance

Questions & Answers

AS exam-style questions

A-level exam-style questions

■ Getting the most from this book

Exam tips

Advice on key points in the text to help you learn and recall content, avoid pitfalls, and polish your exam technique in order to boost your grade.

Knowledge check

Rapid-fire questions throughout the Content Guidance section to check your understanding.

Knowledge check answers

1 Turn to the back of the book for the Knowledge check answers.

Summaries

■ Each core topic is rounded off by a bullet-list summary for quick-check reference of what you need to know.

Exam-style questions

Commentary on the questions

Tips on what you need to do to gain full marks, indicated by the icon **e**

Sample student answers

Practise the questions, then look at the student answers that follow.

Commentary on sample student answers

Find out how many marks each answer would be awarded in the exam and then read the comments (preceded by the icon **e**) following each student answer. Annotations that link back to points made in the student answers show exactly how and where marks are gained or lost.

Section A: core studies

■ AS exam-style questions

Section A: core studies

1 Describe two ways participants were deceived in Bocchiaro et al.'s study into disobedience and whistleblowing. [4 marks]

e The question injunction is 'describe' so these are AO1 marks. You need to demonstrate your understanding of how the Bocchiaro study deceived participants. You are not expected to provide more than 4 minutes of writing.

Student A

The participants were deceived because they were told that the experimenter was investigating the effects of sensory deprivation and that a recent experiment in Rome had harmed participants, some of whom had hallucinations, but this deception because no such experiment had taken place.

Participants were deceived because they were told that they were writing a statement about the research into sensory deprivation that would be mailed to the list of students whose names they had given, but this was untrue as the researchers were only interested in whether the participant blew the whistle or not.

e 4/4 marks awarded. Student A leaves nothing to chance and the description is accurate, thorough and coherent. In one way the participants were deceived is identified and described accurately. In a second way that participants were deceived is identified and described accurately. This is a thorough A-grade answer.

Student B

The participants were deceived because they were told that the experimenter was investigating the effects of sensory deprivation which was not true.

Participants were deceived because they were told that a university ethics committee would be sent their feedback but this was not true.

e 2/4 marks awarded. In Student B has very briefly identified sources of deception but has not described why these were 'deceptions'. This is a probable C/D-grade answer.

2 Bandura's study of transmission of aggression gathered quantitative data. Explain one advantage of gathering this type of data in this study. [3 marks]

e The question injunction is 'explain' so these are AO3 marks. You need to demonstrate your understanding of how/why quantitative data were an advantage in the Bandura study. You are not expected to provide more than 4 minutes of writing.

■About this book

This book is a guide to **Component 2: Psychological themes through core studies** of the OCR AS and A-level psychology specifications. It is intended as a revision aid rather than as a textbook. Its purpose is to summarise the content, to explain how the content will be assessed, to look at the type of questions to expect and to consider sample answers.

There are two sections:

■ **Content Guidance.** This takes you through the material that you need to cover for Component 2: Psychological themes through core studies. There are subsections on the areas, debates, key themes and core studies with which you need to be familiar as well as guidance on the different tasks that might be set in the Component 2 examination.

■ **Questions & Answers.** This section provides sample questions and answers that are followed by comments and marks. Look at the responses and comments on the responses and try to apply the best techniques to your own answers.

In this guide the psychological themes through core studies are organised into **ten key themes** within **five psychological areas (approaches)**. For each of the areas and key themes the following are provided:

■ A synopsis of the area, perspectives, debates and core studies relevant to each area and key theme. This is not intended as the *only* appropriate content but gives you an idea of what you might include in answer to a question on a particular aspect of the specification.

■ Examples of questions in the style of OCR AS and A-level Component 2 exam questions. Each is accompanied by a brief explanation of its requirements as well as the appropriate breakdown of marks between AO1, AO2 and AO3 skills.

■ An example of an A-grade response to each of these questions, showing how the question might be answered by a strong student.

■ An example of a C/D-grade response to each of these questions, with comments showing where marks have been gained or lost.

The aim of the guide is to help you to improve your skills in answering the types of question you might encounter in examinations. Author names and publication dates have been given when referring to research studies. The full references for these studies should be available in textbooks should you wish to read about or research the topic further.

Getting started

You will need a file (or folder) and some dividers. There are five major sections (the psychological areas) in the specification for this component. Within each of these major sections you will need a sub-section for each key theme and for the core studies, so you could start by dividing your file into these sections. You should also include a section into which you can put all your assessed work (do not throw it away — keep it and revise from it, rewriting any answers that did not get full marks). You will learn a great deal from this and it would be advisable to keep all this material together.

The specification

Component 2: Psychological themes through core studies aims to develop critical thinking and independent learning skills through the study of some of the key themes investigated in psychology. Within each key theme there is both a classic and a contemporary core study. The classic studies are research that helped to shape the course of psychology, and each classic study is paired with a contemporary (more up-to-date) study that engages in some way with the issues explored in the classic study.

For each core study you need to learn about:
- how the study relates to its key theme
- how the study relates to the area of psychology it is 'placed' within
- the background or context of the study
- the research method and design
- the sampling method and sample
- any material or apparatus used
- the procedure, results and conclusions

For each pair of studies you need to learn:
- how the two studies are similar
- how the two studies are different
- to what extent the contemporary study changes our understanding of the key theme
- the extent to which the contemporary study changes our understanding of individual, social and cultural diversity

For each core study you must be able to:
- evaluate the strengths and weaknesses of the different research methods and techniques
- evaluate the strengths and weaknesses of different types of data
- evaluate the ethical considerations
- consider validity, reliability, any sampling bias and issues of ethnocentrism

At A-level, the psychological themes through core studies are assessed on Paper 2, which is a 2-hour exam, marked out of 105. At AS, the psychological themes through core studies are assessed on Paper 2, which is a 1½-hour exam, marked out of 75.

On both the AS and the A-level examination paper 10% of the marks available will be for assessment of mathematical skills within the context of psychology. These skills will be at a Level 2 (GCSE level) or higher standard. The specification states that any lower level mathematical skills may still be assessed within examination papers but will not count within the 10% weighting for psychology.

Content Guidance

■ Social psychology

Social psychology focuses on the study of human behaviour within a social context, such as with family, friends, in institutions and culture. Social behaviour may involve activity within a group or between groups.

Psychologists study the way people interact (social interaction) which includes the influence people have on each other. It is important to remember that social influence can be invisible, but that its effects are powerful. One of the assumptions of the social approach is that the people we are with, the social situation, has an effect on the way we behave.

Debate: individual or situational explanations?

A debate in psychology, especially relevant to social psychology, is the extent to which people's behaviour is the result of their individual characteristics (e.g. personality traits) or the result of the situation they are in. Research by social psychologists, for example, by Milgram and Piliavin et al., suggests that the situation people are in does affect behaviour.

The key theme in social psychology at AS and A-level is **responses to people in authority** and at A-level is **responses to people in need**.

In research looking at **responses to people in authority**, Milgram showed that ordinary American men would follow orders from someone they perceived to be a legitimate authority, even to the extent that they would give a fatal electric shock to a stranger. In a more recent study, Bocchiaro et al. found that even when whistleblowing (informing on unethical/immoral behaviour) is easy few people choose to do so.

In research looking at **responses to people in need**, the Piliavin et al. study showed how the situation of the victim may determine whether we offer help, and cross-cultural research by Levine found differences between cultures in whether help is offered to a stranger.

Evaluation

Strengths
- The social approach helps us to understand the influence of the situation in which behaviour is observed, rather than just looking at the characteristics of the person.
- This approach recognises that much behaviour takes place in a social context and helps us to understand how people behave in groups (e.g. jury decision making).
- The approach suggests that if we make changes to social environments we can change people's behaviour.

Weaknesses
- If experimental methods are used, especially laboratory experiments, it is difficult to create an everyday social setting, thus research may lack ecological validity (everyday realism).
- Research may be deterministic and may overestimate situational factors and underemphasise biological factors, individual differences and the role of 'free will'.

Key theme: responses to people in authority (AS and A-level)

Classic study: Milgram (1963) Obedience

Introduction and context

The Milgram study looked at the influence of people who have legitimate authority. Milgram starts his article by referring to the behaviour of German SS officers in the Second World War. He suggests that the people who obeyed the immoral orders were as guilty as those who gave the orders, and that American men would not have followed immoral orders.

Aim and research questions

- Why do people obey authority?
- What are the conditions that foster obedient behaviour?
- What are the conditions that foster independent behaviour?

Research method

An experiment having no independent variable (IV) or a non-naturalistic observation.

Sample

Milgram advertised, using a newspaper and direct mailing, for men to take part in a scientific study of memory and learning at Yale University. Each was paid $4 and travelling expenses. The final participants consisted of 40 men aged between 20 and 50, who came from various occupational backgrounds. There were two further participants: the part of the experimenter was played by a biology teacher, and the part of the learner or victim was a 47-year-old accountant (Mr Wallace).

Procedure

When the participants arrived they were told that the experiment was looking at how punishment affected learning. Each participant drew lots with Mr Wallace (the stooge) to see who would play the part of the teacher and who the learner, but the draw was 'fixed' and Mr Wallace always played the learner. Then Mr Wallace was strapped into a chair in the next door room and attached to the electric shock machine. The teacher, who had been given a sample shock to demonstrate that the machine was working, read out a list of word pairs and the learner had to say which of the four was correct. Every time the learner got a question wrong, he was given an electric shock by the teacher and the shocks increased in intensity with each mistake — from 15 V to 450 V. Mr Wallace had recorded a script which gave mainly wrong answers and for each of these the teacher gave him an electric shock. When the shock level reached 300 V the learner pounded on the wall and shouted to be 'let out'. After the 315 V shock the learner pounded on the wall again but after that remained silent. When the teacher felt unsure about continuing, the experimenter used a sequence of four standard 'prods', which were repeated if necessary:

- Prod 1: Please continue.
- Prod 2: The experiment requires that you continue.
- Prod 3: It is absolutely essential that you continue.
- Prod 4: You have no other choice, you must go on.

Exam tip

Make sure you can explain how quantitative and qualitative data were collected.

If the teacher asked whether the learner might suffer permanent physical injury, the experimenter said: 'Although the shocks may be painful, there is no permanent tissue damage, so please go on.'

Results

Over half of the participants (26/40 or 65%) went all the way with the electric shocks. Only nine of the participants (22.5%) stopped at 315 V. The participants showed signs of extreme tension: most of them were seen to 'sweat, tremble, stutter, bite their lips' and some laughed nervously and smiled in a bizarre fashion. Three even had 'full-blown seizures'.

Conclusion

Milgram proposed the concept of an **agentic state** to explain this high level of obedience. In this situation, the participant acts as the 'tool' of the experimenter, passing the responsibility for the consequences of his actions to the experimenter — 'I was only following orders'.

Milgram also concluded that high levels of obedience were caused by the prestige and high social status of Yale (social influence) and when he moved his experiment to a scraggy office obedience levels reduced.

Note: after the experiment all participants were reunited with Mr Wallace, assured there had been no shocks, and told that their behaviour was normal. In a follow-up questionnaire, 84% felt glad to have participated and only one person said he felt sorry he had participated.

Contemporary study: Bocchiaro et al. (2012) Disobedience and whistleblowing

Introduction and context

A whistleblower is a person who informs on someone who is engaging in immoral or illegal behaviour. Milgram improved our understanding of obedience and why people obey legitimate authority but did not add to our understanding of the nature of disobedience.

Aim and research questions

- Who are the people who disobey or 'blow the whistle'?
- Why do they choose to reject social influence and follow a challenging moral path?
- Do they have personal characteristics which differ from those who obey?

Research method

An experiment having no IV — Bocchiaro et al. call it a 'scenario study'.

Sample

149 undergraduate students, 96 women and 53 men, average age 20.8 years, were given 7 euros or course credits; 11 participants had been removed because they were 'suspicious' about the study. A comparison group of 138 similar students was also used.

Knowledge check 1

Describe two ways the participants were deceived in this study.

Exam tip

Make sure you can explain why the Milgram study is a study of social influence.

Procedure

The study took place at the VU University in Amsterdam. Each participant was greeted by a 'stern', formally dressed male researcher and asked to suggest a few names of fellow students. Then the participant was told a 'cover story' as follows:

> The experimenter and a colleague are investigating the effects of sensory deprivation on brain function. A recent experiment in Rome had disastrous effects on 6 participants who all panicked, whose cognitive ability was temporarily impaired, and who experienced visual and auditory hallucinations. 2 of the 6 had asked to stop, but were not allowed to withdraw because of the effect on data validity. All 6 participants said they had had a frightening experience. We want to replicate the study at VU University because scientists think that young brains may be more sensitive to sensory deprivation. A university research committee is evaluating whether to approve the study and is collecting feedback from students who know the details of the study.

Participants were asked to write a statement, using the words 'exciting, incredible, great and superb' but not mentioning the negative effects of sensory deprivation, to convince the students whose names they had previously given to participate in the experiment. They were told that the statements would be sent to the students by mail. Each participant was also told that if he or she believed that the proposed research on sensory deprivation violated ethical rules he or she could challenge it by putting a form in the mailbox. The experimenter left the room and the participant was taken into the next room where there was a computer on which to write their statement, a mailbox and the research committee feedback forms. After 7 minutes the participant was taken back into the first room, completed two personality tests and questioned about 'any suspicions'. The participants were then fully debriefed, and asked to sign a second consent form. The procedure lasted about 40 minutes.

A group of 138 comparison students from the VU University were provided with a detailed description of the experimental setting. They were then asked 'What would you do?' and 'What would the average student at your university do?'

Results

Who said/did what?	Would obey?	Would disobey?	Would whistleblow?
Comparison group — myself	3.6%	31.90%	64.50%
Comparison group — others	18.80%	43.90%	37.30%
Experimental group	76.50%	14.10%	9.40%

Conclusion

There were no differences in terms of religion, gender or personality traits, and people tend to obey authority figures. Behaving in a moral manner is challenging even when it appears to be easy. People are not very good at predicting what they or others will do.

Note: during the debriefing the participants were fully informed the truth about the experiment.

Knowledge check 2

Describe how the participants were deceived in this study.

Exam tip

Think about research methods, samples, ethics, and research aims. Make sure you can explain one similarity and one difference between the Milgram study and the Bocchiaro et al. study.

Key theme: responses to people in need (A-level only)

Classic study: Piliavin et al. (1969) Subway Samaritan

Introduction and context

In 1964 a young woman called Kitty Genovese was fatally stabbed in New York. The police suggested that there were 38 possible witnesses, but no one did anything to help until it was too late. Why did no one help? Psychologists suggested that the lack of help was caused by **diffusion of responsibility** — no one helps because everyone thinks someone else will do it, and the more people there are present, the less responsibility each person feels and therefore the less likely help is to be forthcoming.

Aim and research questions

- To find out whether diffusion of responsibility does apply in all situations, and what other factors might influence helping behaviour.
- To test the hypothesis that 'people who are responsible for their own plight receive less help'.

Research method

A field experiment having an independent design and 103 trials over 2 months.

Sample

The participants were an **opportunity sample** of nearly 4,500 passengers who happened to be on the New York subway (between 59th Street and 125th Street) on weekdays between 11 a.m. and 3 p.m. There were slightly more white people than black people, and on average there were 43 people in the compartment in any one trial. Each trial lasted 7½ minutes. On each trial, a team of four students boarded the train separately. Two female students acted as observers, one male student was a confederate (role model) and the other acted as a victim. There were four different teams, with a black 'victim' in one of the teams.

> **Knowledge check 3**
>
> Explain why this was an opportunity sample.

Procedure

There were two conditions used to test the hypothesis that 'people who are responsible for their own plight receive less help':
- The 'drunk' condition: the victim smelled of alcohol and carried a bottle wrapped in a brown paper bag.
- The cane condition: the victim was limping and carried a cane.

Seventy seconds after the train pulled out of the station, the male victim staggered and collapsed. If no help was offered the role model stepped in to help after either 70 seconds or 150 seconds. The point of this was to see if a 'model' (someone offering help) affected the behaviour of other passengers.

The two female observers recorded how long it took for passengers to help as well as information about the race, gender and location of all the passengers in the compartment and of all those who offered help. The observers also noted any comments overheard as well as who moved away in each condition.

Results

The cane victim received spontaneous help 95% of the time (62/65 trials) whereas the drunk victim was spontaneously helped 50% of the time (19/38 trials).

The cane victim was helped on average within 5 seconds, whereas the drunk victim was helped after 109 seconds. Only 24% of drunk victims were helped before the role model stepped in, whereas 91% of the cane victims were helped before the role model stepped in.

Black victims received less help less quickly, especially in the drunk condition.

Neither race (black or white) was more helpful, but there was a slight 'same race' effect as whites were slightly more likely to help the 'white victim' than the 'black victim'; 80% of the first helpers were males. The more passengers there were near the victim the more likely help was given, thus there was no evidence of 'diffusion of responsibility'.

Conclusion

A **two-factor model** (or theory) may explain why people help or do not help.

- **Factor 1:** an emergency situation creates a sense of empathy (arousal) in a bystander. This empathic arousal is increased if one feels a sense of identity with the victim, or if one is physically close to the victim. The arousal can be reduced by helping (directly or indirectly). It can also be reduced by going away or finding some way of rationalising why you cannot help.
- **Factor 2:** helping behaviour is determined by a cost–reward calculation. If the possible costs are greater than the possible rewards help is less likely.

Contemporary study: Levine et al. (2001) Cross-cultural altruism

Introduction and context

In 1969 when Piliavin et al. carried out their research into helping behaviour in New York they found that a high rate of immediate help to strangers was given by passengers on the New York subway. Some evidence suggests that the rate of helping differs from city to city and that in cities with 'simpatico' characteristics the rate of helping is higher. Simpatico cultures are defined as cultures in which there is pro-active concern with the social wellbeing of others.

Research aim and questions

- Does whether people help strangers vary cross-culturally?
- Do strangers in a non-emergency situation receive more help in some cities than others?
- How does the 'personality' of a city relate to helping behaviour?

Research method

Field experiments having independent design — 23 field experiments in which there were three types of spontaneous, non-emergency helping, thus three independent variables:

- alerting a pedestrian who dropped a pen
- offering help to a pedestrian with a hurt leg who is trying to reach a pile of dropped magazines
- assisting a blind person to cross the street

The dependant variable (DV) is the rate of helping calculated to give each city a 'helping index'.

Knowledge check 4

What is meant by the term diffusion of responsibility?

Exam tip

Make sure you can identify two factors that might explain why there was no diffusion of responsibility in the Piliavin et al. study.

Sample

Opportunity samples of adults in 23 cities: Vienna, Rio de Janeiro, Sofia, Shanghai, San Jose, Prague, Copenhagen, San Salvador, Budapest, Calcutta, Tel Aviv, Rome, Lilongwe, Kuala Lampur, Mexico City, Amsterdam, Bucharest, Singapore, Madrid, Stockholm, Taipei, Bangkok, New York.

Procedure

- **The researchers:** in most cities, one local individual, usually a student, collected the data. All experimenters were college age and dressed neatly and casually. To control for experimenter gender effects and to avoid potential problems in some cities, all experimenters were men.
- **Dropped pen:** at walking pace experimenters walked towards a pedestrian (214 males and 210 females) walking alone and dropped a pen. Helping was recorded if the pedestrian alerted the researcher that the pen had been dropped or if the pen was picked up and handed over.
- **Hurt leg:** walking with a heavy limp and wearing a visible leg brace, experimenters accidentally dropped and struggled to reach down for a pile of magazines as they came within 20 feet of a passing pedestrian. A total of 253 men and 240 women were approached. Helping was defined as offering to help and/or beginning to help.
- **Helping a blind person cross the street:** wearing dark glasses, and carrying a white cane, the researcher pretended to need help crossing a busy street corner with traffic lights and a pedestrian crossing. They waited until before the light turned green and held out their cane as if asking for help. In total, 281 trials were carried out. Helping was scored if pedestrians, as a minimum, told the researcher when the light was green. If no one helped within 60 seconds, or by the time the light turned red, the researcher walked away from the corner.

Results

The table shows the rate of helping in the top 8 and bottom 8 cities.

Rank order (% helping)							
Rio de Janeiro	San Jose	Lilongwe	Calcutta	Vienna	Madrid	Copenhagen	Shanghai
93.3	91.3	86	82.7	81	79.3	77.7	76.7
1	2	3	4	5	6	7	8
Tel Aviv	Rome	Bangkok	Taipei	Sofia	Amsterdam	Singapore	New York
68	63.3	61	59	57	53.6	48	44.7
16	17	18	19	20	21	22	23

There was a significant positive correlation between the help given in each of the three helping measures in each city.

Conclusion

Richer countries (cities) are less helpful. Cities with simpatico cultures are more helpful. Fast-paced cities (e.g. New York) are less helpful.

Note: the 23 **countries** were Austria, Brazil, Bulgaria, China, Costa Rica, Czech Republic, Denmark, El Salvador, Hungary, India, Israel, Italy, Malawi, Malaysia, Mexico, The Netherlands, Romania, Singapore, Spain, Sweden, Taiwan, Bangkok, USA.

Knowledge check 5

Explain what is meant by a 'simpatico culture'.

Knowledge check 6

Outline how Levine et al. investigated helping behaviour.

Exam tip

Make sure you can explain how this study relates to the key theme of 'responses to people in need' and why this study is 'social psychology'.

■Cognitive psychology

The cognitive approach focuses on internal, mental explanations of behaviour. Cognitive explanations assume that conscious mental processes such as those involved in perception, attention, language, memory and thinking explain behaviour. Cognitive psychologists look at how we input, store and retrieve information and focus on revealing the way that mental or cognitive processes work.

In this topic you study two key themes — attention and memory. At AS and A-level, you study research into **memory**. In the core studies, Loftus and Palmer looked at why eyewitness memory may be unreliable and Grant et al. looked at context-dependent memory. At A-level you study research into **attention**. Moray studied auditory attention and Simons and Chabris studied visual attention.

Assumptions of the cognitive approach

- That behaviour can largely be explained in terms of how the mind operates.
- That the mind works like a computer, inputting, storing and retrieving data.
- That people make decisions as to how they behave.

Debate: free will or determinism?

A debate that is especially relevant to cognitive psychology is the extent to which people's behaviour is the result of unseen mental processes, such as decision making. In other words, the extent to which people have the **free will** to choose their own behaviour. Some psychologists argue that much human behaviour is predetermined by factors such as social influence or biology.

Evaluation

Strengths

- The cognitive approach has useful applications, ranging from advice about the validity of eyewitness testimony to how to improve performance in situations requiring close attention (such as air traffic control), and successful therapies for psychological problems such as stress.
- The approach is not deterministic and it allows that humans have free will to make decisions about their behaviour.

Weaknesses

- The cognitive approach tends to ignore social, motivational and emotional factors and assumes that humans are rational animals, which may underemphasise the role of social influence and human emotion.
- Much research by cognitive psychologists is experimental and based in laboratories in situations that lack ecological validity. For example, many memory experiments measure 'memory for facts', but there are many different kinds of memory.
- Mental processes are essentially private and can be difficult to reveal in 'non-experimental' research.

Key theme: memory (AS and A-level)

Classic study: Loftus and Palmer (1974) Eyewitness testimony

Introduction and context

Memory is not like a camera, it is reconstructive. Elizabeth Loftus has conducted much research investigating the accuracy of eyewitness testimony and the factors that affect eyewitness memory.

Research aim and questions

- To investigate the effect of leading questions on eyewitness memory.
- To investigate whether leading questions distort (change) an eyewitness memory of an event.
- **Hypothesis:** that the strength of the verb used in the leading question (contacted, hit, bumped, collided, smashed) will have a significant effect on participant estimates of the speed of the crash.

Research method

Two laboratory experiments, each having an independent design.

Sample

- **Experiment 1:** 45 students from a university in Washington (USA), randomly allocated to five groups of nine.
- **Experiment 2:** 150 students, randomly allocated to three groups of 50.

Procedure

Experiment 1: 45 student participants watched a video of a car accident (the video was part of a driver safety film). Afterwards the participants were asked to write an account of what they had seen, and then given a questionnaire which included the *critical leading question*: 'How fast were the cars going when they ******* into each other?' The participants were divided into five groups and each group received a different version of the critical question, containing the verb 'contacted', 'hit', 'bumped', 'collided' or 'smashed'. As shown in Figure 1, the leading question did affect participants' perception of speed.

Experiment 2: 150 student participants, in three groups of 50, were shown a film of a car accident and were given a questionnaire. Group 1 were asked the leading question containing the word 'hit', group 2 were asked it with the word 'smashed' and group 3 (the control group) were not asked a leading question. A week later the participants returned and were asked some further questions, including the critical question 'Did you see any broken glass?' (there had been no broken glass in the film).

As shown in Figures 1 and 2, those participants who thought the car was travelling faster (the 'smashed' group) were more likely than the others to produce a false memory of seeing broken glass. This suggests that their memory of what they had seen was changed by the way they had been questioned.

Knowledge check 7

Outline the sample used in the study and suggest one way in which this sample may be biased.

Results

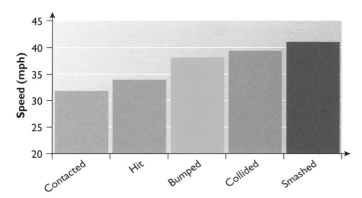

Figure 1 Estimated speed by verb use

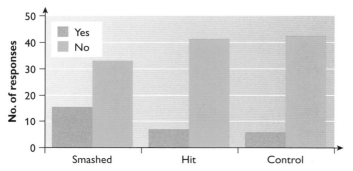

Figure 2 Response to 'Did you see any broken glass?'

Exam tip

Make sure you can explain why this study is categorised as cognitive psychology.

Conclusion

Loftus and Palmer concluded that the meaning of the verb used in the leading question (the semantics of the question) had become integrated with the memory of the event, thus changing the memory and causing a false memory to be constructed. We can also conclude that what happens after we have witnessed an event can alter our memory of the event.

Knowledge check 8

Explain why the use of a control group in experiment 2 increased experimental validity.

Contemporary study: Grant et al. (1998) Context-dependent memory

Introduction and context

Loftus and Palmer showed that the way witnesses are questioned can affect what they remember, but do we remember information we have learned better in the context (environment) in which we learned it?

Research aim and questions

- To investigate whether context cues are important when remembering newly learned information.
- To investigate whether learned information is remembered better in a matching environment than in a non-matching environment.

Research method

A laboratory experiment having an independent measures design.

Sample

A group of 39 students from Iowa state university aged 17–56, 17 females and 23 males.

Procedure

Students were tested one at a time. There were eight experimenters and four experimental conditions:

- learn in silence, recall in silence (matching environment)
- learn in silence, recall in noise (non-matching environment)
- learn in noise, recall in noise (matching environment)
- learn in noise, recall in silence (non-matching environment)

The participants in all conditions wore headphones:

- In the noisy condition participants heard a recording of the noise in the cafeteria consisting of occasional distinct words or phrases amid a general conversational noise mixed with the sounds produced by movement of chairs and dishes. The tape was played at a moderately loud level.
- In the silent condition participants heard nothing.

The participants read a 2-page article on psychoimmunology (Hales 1984), having been told they would be tested on the material. They were allowed to highlight or underline as they usually would. The test involved 10 short-answer questions (maximum score = 10) and 16 multiple-choice questions (maximum score = 16).

The time taken to read the article was recorded in minutes for each participant. There was a 2-minute break between reading the article and the start of the test. The participants were randomly allocated to each of the four conditions.

Results

		Study–test			
		Silent–silent	Silent–noisy	Noisy–noisy	Noisy–silent
Mean	**Reading time**	15	11.8	14	13.8
	Short answer	6.7	4.6	6.2	5.4
	Multiple choice	14.3	12.7	14.3	12.7

As measured by short-answer questions, and by multiple-choice questions, in both the noisy and silence conditions, more information was remembered in the matching conditions than in the non-matching recall conditions.

Conclusion

Context cues appear to be important in the retrieval of newly-learned information. This suggests that students may perform better in exams by studying in silence.

Knowledge check 9

Outline the experimental conditions in the Grant et al. study of contexted memory.

Exam tip

Make sure you can identify the research method used in the Grant et al. study of contexted memory, and are able to explain one advantage of using this research method.

Key theme: attention (A-level only)

Classic study: Moray (1959) Auditory attention

Introduction and context

Can we pay attention to two streams of information at the same time? In a dichotic listening test, a participant is presented with two different auditory stimuli simultaneously (usually speech) into the ears over headphones and then asked to repeat (shadow) the words they hear in one ear. Cherry (1953) introduced the method of 'shadowing' one of two dichotic messages and found that subjects who shadowed a message presented to one ear could recall little or none of the content of a message simultaneously presented to the other ear.

Research aim and questions

- To find out whether participants can remember the content of messages presented to the 'non-attended' ear in a dichotic listening task in which participants are asked to shadow the message presented to one ear.

Research method

Three laboratory experiments.

Sample

Male and female undergraduate students and researchers.

Procedure

Participants practise shadowing a short passage spoken at about 150 words a minute.

Experiment 1: a short list of simple words was presented 35 times (repeated) to one ear of the participant while he or she shadowed a prose message presented to the other ear. After 30 seconds the participant was asked to recall the words presented in the non-attended message.

Findings: when the short list of simple words was presented as the non-attended message there was no trace of the words being remembered even when presented many times.

Experiment 2: participants were asked to shadow ten short passages of fiction making as few mistakes as possible. Instructions such as 'listen to your right ear', 'listen to your right ear — you will receive instructions to change ears' were given at the start of the passages. In six of the passages instructions were given within the passage such as 'change to your other ear' and half of these instructions were prefaced by the participants name – e.g. 'John Smith, you may stop now'.

Findings: when the instruction was given in the non-attended message, participants heard 20 of the 39 times when **the instruction was preceded by their name**, but they heard only 4 of the 36 times when the instruction was not preceded by their name.

Experiment 3: two groups of 14 participants shadowed one of two simultaneous dichotic messages. In some of the messages, towards the end of the message digits (numbers) were included, sometimes in only one message and sometimes in both. One group of participants was told they would be asked questions about the content of the message, the other group was asked to remember as many of the numbers as they could.

> **Knowledge check 10**
>
> Describe the procedure of the attention task in the first experiment.

Findings: there was no significant difference in the number of digits recalled in either condition.

Conclusion

- In a situation where a participant pays attention to a message from one ear, and rejects a message from the other ear, almost none of the content of the rejected message is able to penetrate the attention block.
- Subjectively important messages, such as a person's own name, can penetrate the attention block so that a person will hear instructions if he or she is presented with his or her own name as part of the rejected message.
- It is difficult to make neutral material, such as numbers, important enough to break through the block set up in dichotic shadowing.
- Below the level of conscious perception, a sound pattern which is important to the participant (such as the person's name) is heard, even when he or she is not paying conscious attention to the message.

> **Exam tip**
> Make sure you can apply the findings of the Moray study to explain how to catch someone's attention.

Contemporary study: Simons and Chabris (1999) Visual inattention

Introduction and context

Research into visual attention reveals that we often do not detect large changes to objects and scenes. Furthermore, unless we are paying attention we may not even perceive objects at all.

Research aim and questions

- What role does attention play in visual perception?
- To what degree are the details of our visual world perceived and represented?

Research method

A laboratory experiment having an independent design.

> **Exam tip**
> Make sure you can describe the advantages and disadvantages of volunteer samples.

Sample

Participants were a volunteer sample of 228 observers, mostly undergraduate students. Each participant volunteered without reward, received sweets, or was paid a single fee.

Procedure

Four videotapes, 75 seconds long, were created. Each tape showed two teams of three basketball players, one team wearing white shirts and the other wearing black shirts, who moved around in an open area in front of a bank of three elevator doors passing a standard orange basketball to one another. The passes were either bounce passes or aerial passes — players only incidentally looked directly at the camera.

After 44–48 seconds, either of two unexpected events occurred:

- The umbrella-woman condition: a tall woman holding an open umbrella walked from off camera on one side of the action to the other, left to right.
- The gorilla condition: a person wearing a gorilla costume walked through the action in the same way.

Each unexpected event lasted 5 seconds, and the players continued their actions during and after the event.

There were two styles of video:

■ The **transparen**t condition, in which the white team, black team and unexpected event were all filmed separately, and the three video streams were rendered partially transparent and then superimposed by using digital video-editing software.

■ In the **opaque** condition, all seven actors were filmed simultaneously and could thus occlude one another and the basketballs.

Thus there were four conditions: transparent/umbrella woman; transparent/gorilla, opaque/umbrella woman; and opaque/gorilla.

All observers were tested individually and gave informed consent in advance. Before the viewing, observers were told that they should pay attention to either the team in white (the white condition) or the team in black (the black condition). They were told that they should keep either a silent mental count of the total number of passes made by the attended team (the easy condition) or separate silent mental counts of the number of bounce passes and aerial passes made by the attended team (the hard condition). Thus there were four task conditions: white/easy; white/hard; black/easy; and black/hard. Each observer participated in only one condition.

Observers were then asked a series of questions, including the critical question 'Did you see a gorilla [or a woman carrying an umbrella] walk across the screen?'

Results

The table shows the number of participants in each condition who responded YES to the question 'Did you see a gorilla [or a woman carrying an umbrella] walk across the screen?'

	Easy task		Hard task	
	White team	Black team	White team	Black team
Transparent				
Umbrella woman	58	92	33	42
Gorilla	8	67	8	25
Opaque				
Umbrella woman	100	58	83	58
Gorilla	42	83	50	58

Out of 192 observers 46% failed to notice the unexpected event. (Data from 36 observers was discarded for various reasons).

Conclusion

If we are paying close attention to one aspect of our environment we may not notice quite large objects nearby (inattentional blindness).

Knowledge check 11

Give one example of the results from the Simons and Chabris study and explain it in terms of visual inattention.

Exam tip

This study of visual inattention is a laboratory experiment. Make sure you can describe one advantage and one disadvantage of conducting studies of attention in the laboratory.

■ Developmental psychology

Developmental psychologists focus on changes which take place in individuals throughout their lifetime and on trying to explain why they happen. Development is the sequence of changes that occur over a person's lifetime.

Debate: nature or nurture?

A debate in psychology, relevant to developmental psychology, is the extent to which changes in behaviour are the result of innate biological factors, such as genetic inheritance or brain structure, or whether environmental factors, such as upbringing and/or culture, influence behaviour. Developmental psychology shows that many of the changes are due to inherited factors and maturation (nature). However, a major contribution also comes from the influence of other people and the physical environment (nurture).

There are many aspects to a person's development, for example:

■ cognitive development, which includes increasing one's knowledge and understanding of the world, and learning language
■ social development, for example, moral development, making friends and learning pro- and antisocial behaviour

In this topic you study research from two key themes — **external influences on children's behaviour** and **moral development**. At AS and A-level, the studies that look at external influences on children's behaviour are from the **behaviourist perspective**: the Bandura et al. 'bobo doll' study which looks at the influence of role models to explain the development of aggressive behaviour, and the Chaney et al. Funhaler study. At A-level, the studies on the theme of moral development are both from the cognitive approach: Kohlberg's theory of staged moral development, and the Lee et al. study of evaluations of lying and truth telling.

Evaluation

Strengths
■ The developmental approach helps us to identify changes which are common to most people and to understand and predict age-related changes in aspects of behaviour. For example, theories of cognitive development can be applied to help improve teaching and learning situations in schools.
■ By understanding changes that take place in most people, we can identify abnormal or dysfunctional development.
■ Longitudinal methods can be used to monitor the long-term effect of an experience.

Weaknesses
■ If longitudinal research methods are used, it is difficult to control other factors that can also affect what we are measuring, reducing the validity of research conclusions.
■ Whether longitudinal or cross-sectional methods are used, large samples are required in order to be able to generalise findings to the research population.
■ Longitudinal methods require many participants and researchers as either may move or withdraw. They also require long-term funding.
■ The developmental approach may be reductionist because it may overestimate the influence of age as a cause of behaviour change and ignore other factors such as social or situational influences on behaviour.

The behaviourist perspective

The assumption of behaviourist psychology is that all behaviour is learned — that experience and interaction with the environment make us what we are because we learn stimulus-response units of behaviour in reaction to the environment. This perspective has been called **environmental determinism** because behaviour is determined by past experience.

Radical behaviourism takes the view that all behaviour is learned, but these days most behaviourists take a less radical view. **Neo-behaviourism** is an extension of behaviourism, and the best-known example is **social learning theory** in which Albert Bandura extends learning theory to include a role for cognitive factors, such as perception, attention and memory.

Assumptions of the behaviourist perspective

- That humans and non-human animals are only quantitatively different, and that behaviourists can generalise from research on non-human animals (such as rats and pigeons) to human behaviour.
- That there is no need to look at what goes on inside the 'black box' of the mind (e.g. perception, attention, language, memory, thinking and so on), psychologists need only be concerned with external and observable behaviour.
- That all behaviour can be explained in terms of conditioning theory through classical and/or operant conditioning to produce stimulus and response (S-R) links which build up to produce more complex behaviours. According to behaviourist psychologists we learn by one of three ways — classical conditioning, operant conditioning and social learning.
- That we are born as a blank slate upon which stimulus-response (S-R) units of behaviour are built.

Debate: usefulness of research

Behaviourism has given rise to many practical applications, such as treatments for dysfunctional behaviour, where desirable behaviours are rewarded. The principle is that, if abnormal behaviour (such as a depression, phobia) is learned then it can be unlearned. However, the use of behaviourist therapies to control and change behaviour (as in prisons and psychiatric institutions) could be considered unethical.

Evaluation

Strengths
- Classic learning theory has had a major influence on all branches of psychology.
- Behaviourism has given rise to practical therapies.

Weaknesses
- It is a mechanistic (machine-like) perspective which ignores consciousness, subjective experience and emotions. We are 'puppets' on the strings of our past experience.
- It excludes the role of cognitive (mental) factors (except for social learning theory).

- It denies the role of innate factors.
- It is deterministic: behaviour is determined by the environment and by past experience. It implies that humans are passive in response to their environment.
- It is reductionist: it reduces complex behaviour to stimulus-response units of behaviour.
- It is largely based on work with non-human animals.

Key theme: external influences on children's behaviour (AS and A-level)

Classic study: Bandura et al. (1961) Transmission of aggression

Introduction and context

Behaviourists believe that *all* behaviour can be explained in terms of what people learn by associating a stimulus (S) with a response (R). Bandura felt that cognitive activity does contribute to learning. He suggested that animals and humans learn through both direct *and* indirect experience and that, as children and adults, we observe the behaviour of others and imitate some of these behaviours.

Research aim and questions

- To find out whether aggressive behaviour is learned through imitation.
- If aggressive behaviour is learned by observation, do observers imitate the specific aggressive acts they have seen or do they just become more aggressive?

Research method

A field experiment having a matched participant design.

Sample

Children from a university nursery school (Stanford), 36 boys and 36 girls aged between 37 and 69 months (approximately 3 to 5 years). The mean age was about 4½ years. There were two adult 'models', a male and a female, plus a female experimenter.

Procedure

The matching process. To ensure that each group contained equally aggressive children, observations were done of the children beforehand by two experimenters who knew the children well. They rated the children's physical aggression, verbal aggression, aggression towards inanimate objects and 'aggressive inhibition'. Each child had 4 marks which were then added together to give an aggression score.

Phase 1: the model (exposure to aggression). Each child was taken to a room with toys including a 5-foot inflatable Bobo doll and a mallet. The experimenter invited the 'model' to join them and then left the room for about 10 minutes.

There were three conditions (with 24 children in each):

- **Non-aggressive condition:** the model played with the toys in a quiet manner.
- **Aggressive condition:** the model spent the first minute playing quietly then spent the rest of the time being aggressive, by sitting on Bobo and punching Bobo on the nose, hitting Bobo on the head with the mallet, throwing Bobo in the air. This was done three times along with comments such as 'POW' and 'He sure is a tough fellow'.
- **Control group:** the children were not exposed to a model.

Phase 2: the arousal phase. The children were taken to a room with attractive toys and told that they could not play with the toys. This was necessary because otherwise the children in the non-aggressive condition would have no reason to behave aggressively in Phase 3.

Phase 3: tests for imitation. The children were taken to another room which contained some aggressive toys (e.g. a mallet and a dart gun), some non-aggressive toys (e.g. dolls and farm animals) and a 3-foot Bobo doll. The experimenter stayed with the child while he or she played for 20 minutes, during which time the child was observed through a one-way mirror by the male model and, some of the time, another observer. The observers used a time sampling observation to record what the child was doing every 5 seconds, using the following measures:

- imitation of physical aggression
- imitation of verbal aggression
- imitative non-aggressive verbal responses
- non-imitative physical and verbal aggression

Results

- **Imitation:** children in the aggressive condition imitated many of the model's physical and verbal behaviours, both aggressive and non-aggressive behaviours. Children in the non-aggressive condition displayed very few of these behaviours.
- **Non-imitative aggression:** the aggressive group displayed much more non-imitative aggression than the non-aggressive group.
- **Non-aggressive behaviour:** children in the non-aggression condition spent more time playing non-aggressively and also spent more time just sitting and playing with nothing.
- **Gender:** boys imitated more physical aggression than girls but not verbal aggression. There was some evidence of a 'same-sex model effect' — boys were more aggressive if they watched a male model and girls were more affected by a female model.

Conclusion

Children can learn aggressive behaviour by observing adults behaving aggressively. Learning can take place in the absence of either classical or operant conditioning because children imitated the model's behaviour (learned aggression) in the *absence* of any rewards.

Knowledge check 12

The arousal phase upset the children and was unethical. Why did Bandura et al. think this was necessary?

Exam tip

Revise the difference between time sampling observations and event sampling observations.

Knowledge check 13

Describe how the transmission of aggression was measured in the Bandura et al. study.

Contemporary study: Chaney et al. (2004) Funhaler study

Introduction and context

From the behaviourist perspective, operant conditioning is a form of learning in which behaviour that brings about a rewarding response is likely to be repeated. Children who are asthmatic are often prescribed inhalers, but adherence rates to using them correctly with appropriate frequency are low — from 30% to 70%. The consequences of poor adherence are serious because irregular treatment and poor inhalation technique are linked to more hospitalisation. Improving adherence rates will improve outcomes for asthmatic children.

Research aim and questions

- Can behaviourist techniques, such as operant conditioning and positive reinforcement, be used to improve the treatment of children with asthma?

Research method

A field experiment (carried out in participant homes) having a repeated measures design. The IV was whether the child used a standard inhaler or an inhaler with the Funhaler spacer device.

Sample

A total of 32 children (10 male, 22 female; age range 1.5–6 years, mean age 3.2 years; average duration of asthma of 2.2 years) all of whom were prescribed drugs delivered by inhaler and a new spacer device were recruited into the study with informed consent. Matched questionnaires were completed with 27–32 valid responses to each pair of questions being collected after sequential use of the normal inhaler or the Funhaler for 2 weeks.

Procedure

The standard inhaler and Funhaler devices were compared to ensure they delivered the same amount of the drug. The Funhaler has a whistle that sounds and a spinner/ball that rolls when the inhaler is used correctly. These 'toys' amuse the children and provide positive reinforcement to encourage the children to use the inhaler correctly and make using the inhaler a rewarding experience:

- The children use the standard inhaler for 2 weeks.
- The parents complete questionnaires.
- The children use the Funhaler for 2 weeks.
- The parents complete questionnaires.

Results

- 66% more children took the recommended dose of medication when using the Funhaler than when using the normal inhaler.
- Parents reported significantly more success at medicating their children (22/30 always successful) in comparison to using their existing spacer device (3/30).
- Using the Funhaler was associated with increased child and parent adherence to their recommended treatment plan.

Exam tip

Read your textbook to learn more about classical conditioning, operant conditioning and positive and negative reinforcement.

Exam tip

Thinking about this study, revise the advantages and disadvantages of using self-report methods.

Conclusion

- Improved adherence to medical advice can be achieved if treatment provides a rewarding experience for the children.
- The Funhaler may be a useful device in managing and treating young child asthmatics.
- Behaviourist techniques such as operant conditioning can be used as a way of improving treatment.

Knowledge check 14

What was the external influence that was studied in the Chaney et al. 'Funhaler' study?

Key theme: moral development (A-level only)

Classic study: Kohlberg (1968) Stages of moral development

Introduction and context

Kohlberg's theory of moral development is based on Jean Piaget's maturational stages of cognitive development. Kohlberg proposes that morality changes with age and that there are three levels of moral reasoning — pre-conventional, conventional and post-conventional morality — and that each level consists of two separate stages.

- **Pre-conventional level.** In **Stage 1**, goodness (or badness) is determined by consequences, so that an act is not bad if one can get away with it. In **Stage 2**, children conform to rules in order to gain rewards, and they will do nice things for other people if they think they will benefit.
- **Conventional (conformist) level.** There is an increased understanding of others' intentions, a decrease in egocentrism, and the desire to win praise from others. **Stage 3** is often called the 'good girl/good boy' stage, when children obey rules to gain praise. In **Stage 4** the focus is on the idea that rules should be obeyed because social order and laws are very important.
- **Post-conventional (autonomous) level.** In **Stage 5**, moral actions are those that express the will of the majority (democracy) and maximise social welfare. Finally, **Stage 6** is called universal ethical principles and is marked by a set of self-defined moral principles based on ideas of universal justice and respect for human rights.

Research aim and questions

- Can changes in the development of moral reasoning be measured?

Research method

Longitudinal research using self-report.

Sample

A group of 75 boys from Chicago were followed for 12 years at 3-year intervals. At the start, the boys were aged 10–16 and 58 of them were followed to ages 22–28. Boys in Great Britain, Canada, Taiwan, Mexico and Turkey were also studied.

Procedure

To measure moral reasoning the boys were presented with hypothetical moral dilemmas, such as:

> Heinz's wife was dying from a type of cancer. Doctors said a new drug might save her. The drug had been discovered by a local chemist and Heinz

Exam tip

Make sure you can explain the advantages and disadvantages of longitudinal methods.

tried to buy some, but the chemist was charging ten times the money it cost to make the drug and Heinz could only raise half the money. He explained to the chemist that his wife was dying and asked if he could have the drug cheaper or pay the rest of the money later. The chemist refused, saying that he had discovered the drug and was going to make money from it. The husband was desperate to save his wife, so later that night he broke into the chemist's and stole the drug.

The boys were asked questions such as:

- Should Heinz have stolen the drug?
- Would it change anything if Heinz did not love his wife?
- What if the person dying was a stranger, would it make any difference?
- Should the police arrest the chemist for murder if the woman died?

Results

The results were qualitative data. To determine a child's level of morality, Kohlberg analysed the reasoning behind their answers. For example, in Stage 1 moral reasoning a child might say 'Heinz shouldn't steal the drug because he might go to jail'. In Stage 4, a teenager might say 'Heinz shouldn't steal the drug because stealing is against the law'. In Stage 6, an adult might say 'Heinz should steal the drug because it is his duty to save his wife's life — her life is more important than the law'.

Conclusions

- There are three levels and six stages in the development of moral reasoning and these can be measured.
- People can only pass through the levels in the order listed and each new stage replaces the moral reasoning typical of the earlier stage.
- Not everyone achieves all the stages of moral reasoning.

Contemporary study: Lee et al. (1997) Evaluations of lying and truth telling

Introduction and context

Piaget suggests that children do not begin to consider the intentions that motivate behaviour until they are aged about 11. Kohlberg suggests there are three levels of moral reasoning, having six stages, and that the development of moral reasoning in these stages is the same in all cultures. Sweetser (1987) argues that the understanding of lying is influenced by the cultural norms and moral values in which individuals are socialised.

Research aim and questions

- To compare Chinese and Canadian children's moral evaluations of lying and truth telling in situations involving pro- and antisocial behaviour.

Research method

This is cross-cultural research and is a quasi-experiment having an independent design.

Knowledge check 15

Define qualitative data.

Knowledge check 16

Nature or nurture? Explain which of these Kohlberg concluded caused the development of moral reasoning.

Sample

120 Chinese children: 40 7-year-olds (mean age = 7.5 years, 20 male and 20 female); 40 9-year-olds (mean age = 9.4 years, 20 male and 20 female); 40 11-year-olds (mean age = 11.3, 20 male and 20 female). They were recruited from elementary schools in Hangzhou, Zhejiang Province, a medium-sized city in the People's Republic of China.

108 Canadian children: 36 7-year-olds (mean age = 7.4 years, 20 male and 16 female); 40 9-year-olds (mean age = 9.6 years, 24 male and 16 female); 32 11-year-olds (mean age = 11.5 years, 14 male and 18 female). They were recruited from elementary schools in Fredericton, New Brunswick, Canada.

Procedure

The 7-, 9- and 11-year-old Chinese and Canadian children were presented with four short stories:

■ Two stories involved a child who intentionally carried out a good deed.
■ Two stories involved a child who intentionally carried out a bad deed.

Half of the children were presented with stories that showed a child carrying out a deed directly affecting another child (the social story condition). The other half of the children received stories that showed a child carrying out a deed involving only physical objects (the physical story condition). The children were asked questions about what the child in the story did.

The following is an example of a story that involves a lie in a pro-social setting:

> Here is Alex. Alex's class had to stay inside at recess time because of bad weather, so Alex decided to tidy up the classroom for his teacher.

Question 1: Is what Alex did good or naughty?

> So Alex cleaned the classroom, and when the teacher returned after recess, she said to her students, 'Oh, I see that someone has cleaned the classroom for me.' The teacher then asked Alex, 'Do you know who cleaned the classroom?' Alex said to his teacher, 'I did not do it.'

Question 2: Is what Alex said to his teacher good or naughty?

The children were asked to rate both the story character's deed and verbal statement as 'naughty' or 'good'.

Results

Difference: the Chinese children rated truth telling less positively and lying more positively in pro-social settings than Canadian children, indicating that the emphasis on modesty in Chinese culture overrides evaluations of lying in pro-social situations.

Similarity: both Chinese and Canadian children rated truth telling positively and lying negatively in antisocial situations, reflecting the emphasis in both cultures on the distinction between misdeed and truth/lie telling.

Conclusion

The findings suggest that, as regards lying and truth telling, a close relation between sociocultural practice and moral judgement exists. Specific social and cultural norms have an impact on children's developing moral judgements, which, in turn, are modified by age and experience in a particular culture.

Knowledge check 17

Explain why Lee et al. selected a cross-cultural sample to participate in this study.

Exam tip

This is an example of cross-cultural research. When you learn this study consider the **debates** (i) nature or nurture and (ii) individual explanations or situational explanations.

Knowledge check 18

In terms of the Lee et al. study, explain one advantage of suggesting that behaviour is due to nurture rather than to nature.

Biological psychology

The biological approach assumes that much of our behaviour can be explained in terms of our biological systems. For example, a biological account of stress would focus on how heart rate and breathing increase when in the presence of a stressor. However, it is doubtful whether we can explain all behaviour in terms of biological factors such as brain structure, genes or hormones. The biological approach is said to be reductionist because it reduces the complex nature of human activity to simple systems and ignores the social, cognitive and other factors that have been shown to affect behaviour.

Debate: nature or nurture?

A psychological debate that is especially relevant to biological psychology is the extent to which people's behaviour is the result of innate biological factors, such as genetic inheritance or brain structure, or whether environmental factors, such as upbringing and/or culture, influence behaviour. Some psychologists argue that much human behaviour is predetermined by nature, but recent research has revealed the extent to which nature and nurture interact.

In biological psychology, at AS and A-level, you study research into regions of the brain and brain plasticity. The studies of **regions of the brain** are Roger Sperry's famous study into the effect of the two hemispheres of the brain being surgically separated, and the more recent Casey et al. study that looked at the relationship between biology of the brain and the ability to delay gratification (self-control). At A-level for **brain plasticity**, you look at the Blakemore and Cooper study of the environmental influence on early visual experience, and research by Maguire et al. who found biological changes in the hippocampi (part of the brain) of London taxi drivers.

Assumptions of the biological approach

- That all behaviour can be explained and understood at the level of the functioning of biological systems.
- That there is a direct relationship between the biology of the brain and body and human behaviour.
- That behaviour and experience can be reduced to the functioning of biological systems.

Evaluation

Strengths
- The objective, reductionist nature of biological explanations facilitates experimental research.
- Biological explanations can be used to treat dysfunctional behaviour, as with drug therapies which are widely used to treat mental illnesses often with a reasonable amount of success.
- Biological explanations are scientific because they do not need us to infer metaphysical constructs such as 'mind' to explain human behaviour.

Weaknesses

- Biological explanations offer an objective, reductionist and mechanistic (machine-like) explanation of behaviour, which is oversimplistic.
- The biological perspective overlooks the experiential aspect of behaviour. It ignores past experience in our environment as an influence on behaviour.
- Biological explanations are more appropriate for some kinds of behaviour (such as the physiology of stress), but whether a person feels stressed involves social and psychological factors, therefore biological explanations alone are usually inadequate.
- Biological explanations are deterministic, suggesting that all behaviour is entirely predictable.

Key theme: regions of the brain (AS and A-level)

Classic study: Sperry (1968) Split-brain study

Introduction and context

Our brain has a right and left hemisphere. The right hemisphere controls most of the activity on the *left* side of the body and the left hemisphere controls the *right* side. If you are right-handed the *left* hemisphere is the dominant hemisphere, and language is processed in the *left* hemisphere while spatial awareness and emotion tend to be processed in the *right* hemisphere. Both eyes have a left and right visual field and inputs from the left visual field from both eyes are processed in the *right* hemisphere, and inputs from the right visual field from both eyes are processed in the *left* hemisphere.

Sperry used split-brain patients to find out what happens when the two hemispheres cannot communicate with each other. The split-brain procedure involves cutting the corpus callosum, the largest bundle of nerves which connects the two hemispheres, in an operation called a commissurotomy.

Research aim and questions

- What happens when the two halves of the brain are disconnected?
- Do the hemispheres perform different functions?
- Does each hemisphere have its own memories, perceptions and concepts?

Research method

Laboratory experiments, multiple trials with each participant.

Sample

A volunteer sample of 11 people who all suffered from severe epileptic seizures that could not be controlled by drugs. In each person a commissurotomy had been performed to help their epilepsy.

Procedure

The participant covered one eye and was instructed to look at a fixed point in the centre of a projection screen. Pictures were presented to the left or right visual field by projecting slides onto the right or left of the screen at a very high

Knowledge check 19

Outline one of the ways that Sperry measured the language capability of the left and right hemispheres.

speed, one picture every 0.1 second or faster. Below the screen there was a gap so that the participant could reach objects but not see his or her hands.

Results

- If a picture was first shown to the left visual field, the participant did not recognise it when the same picture appeared in the right visual field.
- If visual material appeared in the right visual field, the patient could describe it in speech and writing.
- If visual material appeared to the left visual field, the patient could identify the same object with their left hand but not their right hand.
- If visual material was presented to the left visual field, the patient consistently *reported* seeing nothing or just a flash of light to their left. However, the participant could point to a matching picture or object with their left hand.
- When two different objects were displayed, e.g. 'case' and 'key', and participants were asked to draw what they saw with their left hand, they drew what was on the left half of the screen (case), but said they had drawn what was on the right half of the screen (key).
- When objects were placed in the *right* hand for identification by touch, participants could describe the object in speech and writing.
- When objects were placed in the *left* hand for identification by touch, participants made wild guesses and seemed unaware of the object in their hand.

Conclusion

When the hemispheres are disconnected, one half of the brain does not know what the other half is doing. The *left* hemisphere (in right-handed people) is specialised for speech and writing and for the organisation of language. It can communicate the visual experiences of the right visual field and the experiences of the right half of the body. The *right* hemisphere is mute and cannot speak or write (is aphasic and agraphic), but can show non-verbally that mental processes, in the left visual field, and the left half of the body, are present.

Contemporary study: Casey et al. (2011) Neural correlates of delay of gratification

Introduction and context

Forty years ago a sample of 4-year-old children performed a delay of gratification task. The children were led into a room where a treat (e.g. a marshmallow) was placed on a table. The children were told they could eat the treat, but if they waited for 15 minutes without giving in to temptation, they would be rewarded with a second treat. Some covered their eyes with their hands or turned around so that they could not see the tray, others started kicking the desk, or stroking the marshmallow as if it were a tiny stuffed animal, while others simply ate the marshmallow as soon as the researchers left. Of those who attempted to delay, one third deferred gratification long enough to get the second marshmallow.

Research aim and questions

- Does the ability to delay gratification as a child predict (a) the ability of adults in their 40s to control impulses and (b) predict sensitivity to social cues (happy faces) at the behavioural and neural level?

Knowledge check 20

Give one example of the behaviour of the split-brain participants that suggests the right hemisphere has no language.

Exam tip

You should be able to suggest a reason why this sample of split brains does not represent the population of normal brains.

Research method

This is a quasi experiment and the independent variable (IV) is whether each participant is a high delayer or a low delayer. The research has a longitudinal design — participants were followed from age 4 to their mid-40s. The research is also a correlational analysis. There are two experiments.

Sample

A group of 562 adults who were 4-year-old children in the 1960s; 155 completed self-control scales in their 20s, and 135 again in their 30s.

Participants in this study were 59 (of the 135) who were 'above or below' average on the original measure of delay of gratification and 'above or below' average in the self-control measure — 32 were high delayers and 27 low delayers; 27 (13 male, 14 female) also agreed to participate in a neuroimaging study.

Procedure

Experiment 1

Go vs no-go impulse control task — there were two versions of the task:
- **Cool version:** the participant is told which gender is the target. There are four conditions: male go, female go, male no-go, female no-go. 160 male or female faces are projected on a screen (one at a time) for 500 milliseconds (ms) with a 1-second interval. Each face has a go/no-go option. The participants are told to press the button for go but not for no-go. Accuracy and reaction times are recorded.
- **Hot version:** the task is the same but the faces are happy or fearful.

Experiment 2

fMRI was used while a similar go vs no-go task is completed:
- The participant is told which gender is the target. 48 male or female faces are projected on a screen (one at a time) either happy or fearful for 500 ms with a 1-second interval. Each face has go/no-go option. The participants are told to press the button for go but not for no-go. Accuracy and reaction times are recorded.
- fMRI imaging of the right prefrontal cortex and the ventral striatum was undertaken for 26 participants.

Results

- Participants who were low delayers as children showed more difficulty as adults in suppressing responses to hot cues (happy faces) than those who were high delayers as children.
- The right inferior frontal gyrus was active when accurately withholding (no-go) responses.
- Compared to the high delayers, the low delayers had less activity in the right inferior frontal gyrus for correct no-go trials.
- The prefrontal cortex (ventral striatum) showed more activity to happy no-go trials in low delayers.

Conclusion

Resistance to temptation as a child is a stable individual difference that predicts (correlates with) biases in brain circuitries that integrate motivation and control.

Individuals who at the age of 4 have difficulty resisting temptation, and who continue to show reduced self-control, have more difficulty as adults in suppressing responses to positive social cues.

Key theme: brain plasticity (A-level only)

Classic study: Blakemore and Cooper (1970) Impact of early visual experience

Introduction and context

In a normal cat, neurons of the visual cortex are selective for the orientation of lines and edges in the whole visual field, but early visual experience can change this orientation. In previous research, kittens were reared with one eye viewing vertical stripes and the other horizontal stripes. Out of 21 neurons, in 20 the orientation of the receptive field matched the pattern of stripes experienced by that eye.

Research aim and questions

- To investigate the influence of early visual experience on the development of the visual system in kittens.

Research method

Laboratory experiment having an independent design.

Sample

Kittens.

Procedure

The kittens were raised from birth in a dark room and at 2 weeks old were put into a special apparatus for 5 hours a day. The kitten stood on a glass table inside a cylinder (no corners, no edges) which was covered with either vertical or horizontal black and white stripes. The kittens could not see their own body because they wore a collar that restricted their visual field. When the kittens were 5 months old, they were taken out of the cylinder and taken into a well-lit room, with tables and chairs, and were observed.

Results

Within 10 hours of being taken out of the cylinder the kittens could jump with ease from a chair to the floor. They were clumsy when chasing moving objects. They often bumped into the table legs or furniture.

The kittens were tested for line recognition. They showed 'behavioural blindness' — those raised in a horizontal environment could not detect vertically aligned objects. Only the eyes of the kittens raised with vertical stripes followed a rod held vertically. When the kittens were 7.5 months old they were anaesthetised while neurons in the visual cortex were studied: 125 neurons from two cats, one horizontally and one vertically exposed, were studied. Horizontal plane neurons did not 'fire-off' in those kittens raised in the vertical environment, and vertical plane neurons did not 'fire-off' in kittens raised in the horizontal environment.

Knowledge check 21

Outline one difference between the Sperry split-brain study and the Casey et al. study of neural correlates of delay of gratification.

Knowledge check 22

Write a brief outline of how the kittens were treated in the Blakemore and Cooper study.

Exam tip

This study raises ethical issues and you should take the opportunity to look at the BPS ethical guidelines relating to research with non-human animals.

Conclusion

The visual cortex may adapt itself to the nature of its visual experience during maturation. This illustrates neural plasticity. While it is an evolutionary advantage for an animal's brain to have hard-wired capacities at birth, such as the ability to respond to lines of certain orientations, it is also an advantage for the brain to be able to adapt to environmental conditions. Cells may change their preferred orientation towards that of the commonest type of environmental stimulus.

Contemporary study: Maguire et al. (2000) Taxi drivers

Background and context

A significant body of research suggests that the role of the hippocampus is to facilitate spatial memory (navigation).

Research aim and questions

- The aim was to find out whether changes in the brain could be detected in people who have extensive navigation experience, specifically to find out whether the hippocampi in London taxi drivers will be structurally different from the hippocampi in non-taxi drivers.

Research method

This is a quasi experiment (natural experiment). The IV was whether it was a London taxi driver (brain) or non-taxi driver (brain). The DV was the structure and volume of the hippocampi.

Sample

A volunteer sample of two groups of people who had applied to be included in the study. Fully informed consent was gained. All had healthy general medical, neurological and psychiatric profiles:

- **Group 1:** 16 right-handed, male 'London Black Cab' taxi drivers, average age 44, all licensed for more than 18 months, average time as taxi driver was 14.3 years.
- **Group 2:** 16 right-handed, male, age-matched non-taxi drivers.

Procedure

Stage 1: MRI scans of brains of 50 healthy, right-handed, male, non-taxi drivers aged 33–61 were analysed to establish a comparison database of 'average hippocampi' (analysis by voxel based morphometry, VBM).

Stage 2: MRI scans of brains of 16 taxi drivers and of 16 matched controls were analysed by VBM and compared to this database.

Control: the expert conducting the analysis did not know whether each MRI scan was of a taxi driver brain or not.

Results

As shown in Figure 1, there was an increased volume of grey matter in both the right and left hippocampi in taxi driver brains, and as shown in Figure 2, correlational analysis found that the volume of grey matter in the posteria hippocampi increased as the length of time as a taxi driver increased. Taxi drivers had greater volume

Knowledge check 23

The study by Blakemore and Cooper looks at an aspect of brain plasticity. Explain what is meant by 'brain plasticity'.

Exam tip

One similarity between the Blakemore and Cooper study and the Sperry split-brain study is that in both studies inferences about the brain were made from observed behaviour. Make sure you can explain what this means.

Knowledge check 24

Explain why Maguire et al. selected taxi drivers to participate in this study.

of grey matter in the posteria hippocampi but non-taxi drivers had greater volume in the anterior hippocampi, indicating a redistribution of the grey matter in the hippocampus.

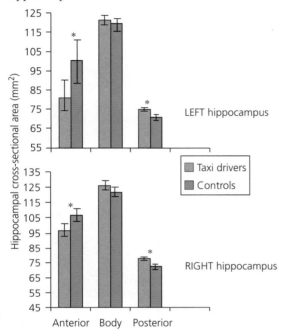

Figure 1

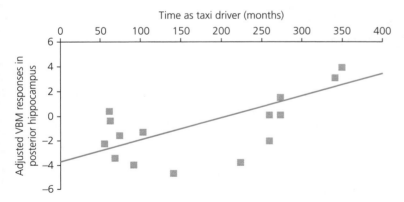

Figure 2

Conclusion

- That the structure of the brain changes in response to environmental demand.
- That the mental map of the city of London is stored in the posteria hippocampi in taxi drivers.
- That normal behaviour can induce changes in the structure of the brain and that this has many implications for rehabilitation after brain injury.

Exam tip

You should be able to explain why Maguire et al. investigated the correlation between the volume of grey matter in the right hippocampi and the length of time each participant had been a licensed taxi driver.

Knowledge check 25

Suggest one difference between the Blakemore and Cooper study of kittens and the Maguire et al. study of taxi drivers.

■ Individual differences

Psychologists need to take account of individual and cultural differences in their theories. Traditionally, many research findings were based on white, middle-class, American males, often students, thus many of the traditional theories in psychology are explanations of the behaviour of a rather biased sample of human beings.

There are many areas of interest and debate within psychology, not least of which is the most fundamental question of 'what is normal', especially when considering explanations for dysfunctional behaviour. The individual differences approach treats each person as a unique individual and often uses case study methodology.

Debate: reductionism or holism?

A debate especially relevant to this topic is to what extent should psychologists try to quantify the single factors that may explain human behaviour rather than taking a holistic approach and looking at all of the influences on a person's behaviour? A case study can be said to be a holistic approach as it is a detailed study into the life and background of one person (or of a small group). Case studies involve looking at past records, such as school and health records, and asking other people about the participant's past and present behaviour.

In this topic you study research from two key themes — **understanding disorders** and **measuring differences**. At AS and A-level, the studies on understanding disorders are from: the **psychodynamic perspective** — the Sigmund Freud case study of Little Hans' phobia of horses; and the **cognitive approach** — the Baron-Cohen et al. study of autism in adults. At A-level, the studies on the theme of measuring difference are both from the cognitive approach: the Gould (1982) study of IQ testing, and the study by Hancock et al. (2011) which looked at the language of psychopaths.

Evaluation

Strengths

- This approach has useful applications, mainly in therapies for treating dysfunctional behaviour. The problem of assessing such therapies is how does one make comparisons? Would the person have recovered anyway, without any treatment? How can one ethically conduct research where some people receive a therapy and others do not?
- Case studies give a very detailed picture of an individual and help to discover how a person's past may be related to their present behaviour.
- By studying unusual behaviour we can learn more about the usual.

Weaknesses

- The approach may be reductionist because it may overestimate the role of individual factors and ignore social and situational influences on behaviour.
- If case study methods are used the findings can only be applied to the person being studied, so findings can never be generalised to explain other people's behaviour.
- Retrospective studies may rely on memory which may be biased or faulty or incomplete and on past records which may be incomplete.

The psychodynamic perspective

The psychodynamic perspective, whose founding father was Sigmund Freud, explains human behaviour in terms of an interaction between innate drives and early experience. Freud wrote that there are three parts to the human psyche (personality):

- The id is the primitive, innate part of personality.
- The ego is the conscious part of personality that regulates the id.
- The super ego is the moral part that is learned from parents and society.

These parts are hypothetical entities (they do not actually exist) and they develop through the five psychosexual stages: oral, anal, phallic, latent and genital.

Assumptions of the psychoanalytic perspective

- That human development is a dynamic process and that early experience drives us to behave in predictable ways.
- That childhood is a critical period of development. Infants are born with innate biological drives and these drives have a physical (sexual) basis.
- If these drives are not satisfied, the ego copes by using ego defence mechanisms (e.g. repression, denial) and thoughts, feelings and behaviour can be influenced as a result.
- Individual personality differences can be traced back to the way early conflicts were handled in infancy and childhood, and these conflicts remain with the adult and unconsciously motivate behaviour.

Evaluation

Strengths
- Freud recognised that childhood is a critical period of development.
- The theory has been enormously influential within psychology, and beyond.
- This approach focuses on the individual rather than on general laws of behaviour. Psychodynamic theory provides a rich picture of individual personality.

Weaknesses
- The theory lacks empirical support (objective research evidence) and where there is 'evidence' this is mostly from case studies of middle-class, European women, many of whom experienced anxiety disorders.
- The data were collected retrospectively and because they were interpreted there is the potential for investigator bias. Also, Freud may have influenced the things his patients said (e.g. case study of Little Hans).
- It reduces human activity to a basic set of abstract concepts (id, ego, super ego) which are presented as if they are real things.
- It is deterministic because it implies that people have little free will and it suggests that adult behaviour is determined by childhood experiences.

Debate: psychology as a science?

The empirical approach (all knowledge comes through our senses) is the scientific approach. The most empirical method of enquiry in science is the experiment. The important features of the experiment are control over variables (independent, dependent and extraneous), careful objective measurement and establishing cause-and-effect relationships. Can psychology be viewed as a science like biology, chemistry and physics? Freud's theories are arguably unscientific as they are 'matters of opinion' rather than 'matters of fact'.

The key features of science

- **Empirical evidence:** data are collected through direct observation or experiments.
- **Objectivity:** researchers remain unbiased in their investigations and all sources of bias such as personal or subjective ideas are eliminated.
- **Control:** extraneous variables need to be controlled in order to be able to establish cause (IV) and effect (DV).
- **Predictability:** scientists should be able to predict future behaviour from the findings of research.
- **Hypothesis testing:** a hypothesis serves as a prediction and is derived from a theory. Hypotheses need to be stated in a form that can be tested (i.e. operationalised and unambiguous).
- **Replication:** if a discovery is reported but it cannot be replicated by other scientists it will not be accepted. Replicability of research is vital in establishing a scientific theory.

Is psychology a science? Most scientific disciplines have one predominant paradigm that almost all scientists subscribe to. Anything with several paradigms (e.g. models or theories) is not a science until the multiple theories are unified. Since psychologists do not have any universal laws of human behaviour, and there are many different paradigms (approaches) within psychology, perhaps psychology is not a science?

Key theme: understanding disorders (AS and A-level)

Classic study: Freud (1909) Little Hans

Introduction and context

This case study of Little Hans (a 5-year-old boy) enabled Freud to test his theory that a young child goes through unconscious psychosexual stages during early development and at around the age of 3 the child enters the phallic stage. During the phallic stage the child's interest focuses on their opposite sex parent. A boy loves his mother and comes to have sexual desires for her. This places him in conflict with his father who now becomes his rival. As a result the boy wishes his father dead, which arouses feelings of guilt. The boy fears that his father will find out his feelings and punish him by castrating him. Freud called this the Oedipus complex and proposed that when the boy resolves the Oedipus conflict he can identify with his father and cease desiring his mother.

Research aim and questions

Little Hans was going through the phallic stage of development and his feelings and behaviour may provide support for Freud's theory. Hans had a phobia of horses and together Hans' father and Freud studied Hans to try to cure this.

Research method

A longitudinal case study.

Sample

A 5-year-old boy called Little Hans. His father was Max Graf, an early supporter of Freud. Hans' father and Freud exchanged letters, the data were collected by Hans' father who wrote to Freud, who interpreted Hans' behaviour and then wrote back with suggestions.

Procedure and findings

Hans' father wrote to Freud when the boy was 5 years old, saying: 'He is afraid a horse will bite him in the street, and this fear seems connected with his having been frightened by a large penis'.

Hans and his 'widdler': Hans had an interest in that part of his body he called his 'widdler'.

Hans' mother and sister: when Hans was 3½ his baby sister was born. He expressed hostility towards his new sister and developed a fear that his mother would drop him when she was bathing him. When his father talked to him about this Hans admitted that he wished his mother would drown his sister. This unconscious desire became translated into a fear that his mother might let Hans drown.

The links between horses and anxiety: Hans' fear was that a white horse would bite him. Freud felt that Hans' real fear was that he would lose his mother. Freud traced the link between these two. Hans had heard a man in the street saying to a child, 'Don't put your finger to the white horse or it'll bite you'. On another occasion, Hans had asked his mother if she would like to put her finger on his widdler but his mother told him this would not be proper.

Hans' castration fear: Hans enjoyed playing with his widdler but when his mother found him doing this she threatened that she would arrange for it to be cut off. This would serve to confirm his fears of castration.

Hans' dreams and fantasies: Hans told his father a dream about two giraffes — a big one and a crumpled one. Hans took away the crumpled one and sat down on it, and this made the big one cry out. This was interpreted as a representation of what happened in the mornings when Hans liked to get into his parents' bed but his father (the big giraffe) objected. Hans took away his mother (the crumpled one) which caused his father to cry out. Hans sat on top of his mother to claim her for himself. Freud wondered if the giraffe's long neck represented the large adult penis.

The link between fear of horses and fear of father: Freud suggested that Hans' fear of horses was actually a fear of his father. The black around the horses' mouths and the blinkers in front of their eyes were symbols for his father's moustaches and glasses.

The resolution: Hans' fear of horses began to subside and Hans developed two final fantasies which showed that he had now resolved his feelings about his father. 'The

Knowledge check 26

Suggest why the Freud study of Little Hans can be viewed as a study of individual differences.

plumber came and first he took away my behind with a pair of pincers, and then he gave me another, and then the same with my widdler'. This is taken to mean that Hans was given a bigger backside and widdler, like Daddy's.

Conclusion

Freud felt the evidence supported his theory of psychosexual development. First, there is clear evidence of Hans' interest in sexual matters. Second, there is also evidence to support the idea of the Oedipus complex and that the successful resolution of this came when Hans was able to express his feelings about his father and was finally able to transfer his identification from his mother to his father.

Contemporary study: Baron-Cohen et al. (1997) Autism in adults

Introduction and context

The term autism is used to describe a wide spectrum of disorders from Asperger syndrome at one end through to individuals showing severe forms of autism at the other extreme. People with Asperger syndrome are often of average or above average intelligence and usually have fewer problems with language. Adults with autistic spectrum disorders have problems with social relationships. Research using first order theory of mind (TOM) tasks found that children diagnosed as autistic are not able to reason what another person is thinking. An example of a first order TOM task is the 'Sally Anne' test. Normal children develop the ability to 'read minds' by the age of 6 but the Sally Anne test is not appropriate for adults. To find out more about the 'Sally Anne' test, look up: www.tinyurl.com/8ydqa35

Research aim and questions

- To investigate why adults with autistic spectrum disorders have problems with social relationships.
- To develop an advanced test for theory of mind in adults with autism.

Research method

A quasi (natural) experiment having a matched participant design.

Sample

Three groups of participants:
- 16 autistic (Asperger): 13 male, 3 female
- 50 normal: 25 male, 25 female
- 10 Tourette's patients: 8 male, 2 female

The sample were matched on age and normal intelligence and the two clinical groups had passed first order TOM tests at 6-year-old level.

The IV was whether participants were normal, autistic or had Tourette's syndrome. The DV was how they performed on the eyes task (maximum score = 25).

Procedure

The 'eyes task' procedure: 25 photos of eyes, each 15 × 10 cm black and white, were each shown for 3 seconds. Participants, tested individually, were asked a forced-choice question. For example: which word best describes what this person is thinking or feeling?

Knowledge check 27

Identify the type of data collected and, with reference to 'Little Hans', explain one advantage of this type of data.

Exam tip

Make sure you can describe one of Hans' dreams or phobias.

Exam tip

You should be able to explain an advantage of using a matched participant design.

Knowledge check 28

Can you suggest why Baron-Cohen et al. selected Tourette's patients to be a control group?

The 'eyes task' was created by selecting magazine photos. Four judges generated the target words, e.g. target = calm, foil = anxious. The target is the correct answer, the foil is the opposite. As a control, the target was presented randomly on both left and right.

Control: when generating targets and foils the eye photos were shown to a panel of eight adults who did not know there was a 'right or wrong' answer and there was 100% agreement with the target. The control tasks included:

- **Gender identification:** all the participants were asked to identify the gender of each of the 25 eye photos.
- **Basic emotion recognition task:** all the participants were asked to identify the emotion in six full-face photos — happy, sad, angry, afraid, surprise, disgust (the *Ekman categories*).

Results

The autistic adults were less likely to identify the correct target than the normal or Tourette's group. The normal and Tourette's scores were significantly better than the autistic group scores.

Eyes task	Autistic	Normal	Tourette's
Mean	16.3	20.3	20.4
Range	10	9	9

Females were better at reading minds from eyes than males. Normal females were significantly better than normal males.

Eyes task	Normal (male)	Normal (female)
Mean	18.8	21.8
Range	6	5

Conclusion

There is evidence for subtle 'mindreading' deficits in intelligent adults on the autistic spectrum. The eyes task is a 'pure theory of mind test' for adults — because there is no context the task does not require an understanding of what the person whose eyes are shown is 'doing'.

Key theme: measuring differences (A-level only)

Classic study: Gould (1982) A nation of morons: bias in IQ testing

Introduction and context

What is intelligence? For over 100 years, psychologists have found it difficult to answer this question and will probably never reach agreement about what it is. But, if we are not sure what intelligence 'is', can we design reliable and valid intelligence tests to measure it? Two questions that psychologists have struggled with are: (a) Is intelligence inherited? and (b) Can intelligence be measured? The very first intelligence tests, designed by Binet, were commissioned as a means of testing French school children who had 'fallen behind' to see who might require special education — Binet believed intelligence could be increased by education.

This study is a review of the history of intelligence testing. The term 'IQ' is the usual test score given in an intelligence test. It stands for 'intelligence quotient', a quotient being the result of a division — mental age (MA, your score on the test) divided by your chronological age (CA). This is done because we would expect a 5-year-old to do less well than a 10-year-old, therefore their scores should be adjusted for their age. The quotient is then multiplied by 100 to get rid of the decimals. So to calculate an IQ score the formula is IQ = MA/CA × 100. IQ scores are norm referenced — that is, the average performance of a group is calculated, then individual scores are compared to this average.

How is IQ calculated?

Example: an 'intelligence' test is devised with a variety of questions suitable for the age of the people being tested. For example, if 10-year-olds are being tested, questions suitable for 8-year-olds, 9-year-olds, 10-year-olds, 11-year-olds and 12-year-olds may be included.

After the child (person) has completed the test, the questions are reviewed. If a 10-year-old has correctly answered all the questions for the 9-year-olds and all the questions for the 10-year-olds but none of the questions for the 11-year-olds, then the mental age (MA) is equal to the chronological age (CA) which is shown in the formula:

$$IQ = MA/CA \times 100$$

MA: mental age

CA: calendar age

So, in the example,

$$IQ = 10/10 \times 100$$

$$IQ = 100$$

If the 10-year-old had correctly answered all the 11-year-old questions, the child's IQ would be calculated as:

$$IQ = 11/10 \times 100$$

$$IQ = 110$$

Research method

A review of the uses of early IQ testing.

Procedural history

In the USA strong supporters of IQ testing were scientists who believed that intelligence is mainly genetic, and that a responsible society should breed a superior group of people. Yerkes was a psychologist who saw possibilities in the field of IQ testing. If you could provide numbers to represent intelligence, this would be extremely useful in society. The advent of the First World War gave Yerkes an opportunity to develop mental testing. He suggested that it might be highly desirable to test all US army recruits so that the most able could be given jobs with greater responsibility. Yerkes got together with other psychologists, such as Terman, and wrote a set of mental tests.

The type of questions they used were:

- *analogies*, such as 'Washington is to Adams as first is to …' [second, because Washington was the first US president and Adams was the second]

Exam tip

Make sure you can explain why some of these questions are culturally biased.

- *filling in the next number in a sequence*, such as 'What number comes next: 1, 3, 6, 10, …'
- *multiple choice*, such as 'Crisco is a: patent medicine, disinfectant, toothpaste, food product?' [It is a food product] or 'The number of a Kaffir's legs is: 2, 4, 6, 8? [The answer is 2 because a Kaffir is an African tribesman]

In 1917 Yerkes and his team tested 1.75 million army recruits using the intelligence tests they had designed. Because not all the army recruits being tested could write they devised two forms of the test:

- The *Army Alpha* test was a written exam.
- The *Army Beta* was a set of pictures. This was given to recruits who failed the Alpha test or who could not read, but it involved *writing* the answers.
- If a recruit failed the Beta test then they were supposed to be tested individually.

Each man was graded from A to E. Grade D men were 'rarely suited for tasks requiring special skill' and could not be expected to 'read and understand written instructions'.

Yerkes said: 'These tests measure "innate intellectual ability" in other words intelligence that is unaffected by culture or education.' As a result of these tests IQ testing became 'scientifically established'.

Outcome of Yerkes' tests

After the war, these tests became widely used by schools and businesses because they could be used to select employees etc. A second area of interest arose from looking at the army data. Boring studied the test results from 160,000 men and drew the following conclusions:

- *White Americans*: the average mental age was only 13, just above being a moron.
- *European immigrants*: they were all 'morons' but those from northern and western Europe were brighter than were those from the east and south.
- *Negroes*: these were at the bottom of the scale, scoring an average of 10.41.
- Different cultural/racial groups differed in terms of their intelligence and those with lower IQ were doomed to remain this way because intelligence was inherited.

However, test scores rose in relation to the number of years an immigrant had lived in the USA (a positive correlation) which suggested that learning not innate intelligence was involved. The tests cannot be seen as valid or reliable. According to Gould, what is frightening is not that intelligent men devised such stupid tests, but that others believed the results without questioning the method by which they were obtained.

Conclusion

- Despite evidence that Yerkes' IQ tests were culturally biased, by 1921 IQ testing was common in business and education.
- There is no good evidence to suggest that IQ differences are the result of genetic differences.
- There is no clear operational definition of intelligence. IQ is a political rather than a biological definition.

Knowledge check 30

Nature or nurture? According to Gould, which of these was being measured by Yerkes' IQ tests?

Knowledge check 31

Suggest two sources of bias that could have affected performance on Yerkes' IQ tests.

Exam tip

You should be able to evaluate Yerkes' IQ tests in terms of validity and reliability.

Contemporary study: Hancock et al. (2011) Language of psychopaths

Introduction and context

Psychopathy can be determined by using the Psychopathy Checklist-Revised (PCL-R). The PCL-R identifies the characteristic traits of psychopaths such as superficial charm, pathological lying, manipulation of others, impulsivity, juvenile delinquency and criminality.

Does the way people speak reflect the way people think and their underlying personality? Psychopaths are described as being emotionally flat, lacking in empathy, free of feelings of guilt and they use deception and 'pretended' emotion to manipulate others. Recent research suggested that much can be learned about these individuals by close examination of their language. If the way people think is reflected in the way they talk then psychopathic speech is predicted to reflect an instrumental/predatory world view, unique socio-emotional needs, and to be emotionless.

Research aim and questions

- Because psychopaths are skilled at manipulating, deceiving and controlling their self-presentation, examining subtle aspects of their language represents a new way to gain insight into their behaviour.
- Can the characteristic traits of psychopaths be found in their speech patterns? This study used statistical text analysis to examine the features of crime narratives provided by psychopathic murderers.

Research method

Content analysis.

Sample

The stories told by 14 imprisoned psychopathic male murderers and those of 38 convicted murderers who were not diagnosed as psychopathic. Each prisoner was asked to describe his crime in detail and then the stories were taped, transcribed and subjected to computer analysis using two text analysis tools.

Procedure

Psychopathy was determined using the Psychopathy Checklist-Revised (PCL-R). The Wmatrix linguistic analysis tool (Rayson, 2008) was used to examine parts of speech and semantic content while the Dictionary of Affect and Language (DAL) tool (Whissell and Dewson, 1986) was used to examine the emotional characteristics of the narratives.

Results

- Psychopaths used more conjunctions like 'because', 'since' or 'so that', implying that the crime 'had to be done' to obtain a particular goal.
- They used twice as many words relating to physical needs, such as food, sex or money, while non-psychopaths used more words about social needs, including family, religion and spirituality.

Exam tip

If you have not yet done so, it would be a good idea to 'read up' on the strengths and limitations of content analysis.

- Psychopaths' speech contained a higher frequency of speech disfluencies (e.g. 'uh', 'um') indicating that describing powerful, 'emotional' events (e.g. a murder) to another person was relatively difficult for them.
- Psychopaths used more past tense and fewer present tense verbs in their narrative, indicating a greater psychological detachment from the incident, and their language was less emotionally intense.

Conclusion

- It might be possible to screen people suspected of violent crimes because knowing a suspect is psychopathic could inform strategies for pursuit or interrogation.
- The psychopath's world view is fundamentally different from the rest of the human species.
- Interviews with suspected psychopaths should be recorded for analysis because to facilitate the identification of an individual as a psychopath, it is important to collect as much language as possible.

Note: Hancock et al. recognise that their analysis applies only to murderers relating the story of their own crimes, and suggest further studies of speech patterns in more neutral situations.

Summary

The table below summarises the core studies and suggests how they are, and/or could be, related to the areas, perspectives, issues and debates.

Study	Area/perspective	Issue/debate
Social psychology		
Milgram (1963) Obedience	**Social:** the results show how social influence from a high status person can influence obedience to the extent that people will potentially kill a stranger	**Situational or individual explanation** Situational — social influence real or imagined does affect behaviour
Bocchiaro et al. (2012) Disobedience and whistleblowing	**Social:** similar to Milgram it revealed high levels of obedience but also sought to investigate whether there are personality differences in obedience/disobedience	**Situational or individual explanation** Situational — social influence real or imagined does affect behaviour but it also considers individual explanations
Piliavin et al. (1969) Subway Samaritan	**Social:** it looked into the impact of other people (diffusion of responsibility) on helping behaviour	**Situational or individual explanation** Situational — explains helping (or not) partly as the response to the 'state' of the victim
Levine (2001) Cross-cultural altruism	**Social:** cross-cultural research investigating helping in non-confined situations in 23 countries	**Situational or individual explanation** Situational — the results found that culture does have an effect on helping behaviour

Cognitive psychology		
Loftus and Palmer (1974) Eyewitness testimony	**Cognitive:** a study of memory showing how post-event information can change memory or even create false memory	**Psychology as a science** Uses scientific methods to reveal mental processes
Grant et al. (1998) Context-dependent memory	**Cognitive:** the study shows that information is remembered better in a similar context to that in which it was learned, and explains how to help people 'remember'	**Psychology as a science** Uses scientific methods to reveal mental processes
Moray (1959) Auditory attention	**Cognitive:** a study of attention. The study looks at what kind of information breaks the attentional barrier	**Psychology as a science** Uses scientific methods to reveal mental processes
Simons and Chabris (1999) Visual inattention	**Cognitive:** the study explains why we perceive but do not remember information that we have not attended to	**Free will or determinism** Do we have the free will to choose what we 'see'?
Developmental psychology		
Bandura et al. (1961) Transmission of aggression	**Developmental:** it shows how children's behaviour can be influenced by the behaviour of adult role models **Behaviourist:** it provides empirical support for social learning theory — the children imitated the aggressive behaviour of the role models	**Situational or individual explanation** Situational — because if no aggressive role models a child will not learn aggressive behaviour **Nature or nurture** Nurture — because aggressive behaviour is learned not innate
Chaney et al. (2004) Funhaler study	**Developmental:** it shows how children's behaviour is influenced by external factors **Behaviourist:** it provides support for operant conditioning (positive and negative reinforcement) in the increased adherence, due to the positive reinforcement provided by Funhaler	**Nature or nurture** Nurture — because it suggests that positive reinforcement changes behaviour
Kohlberg (1968) Stages of moral development	**Developmental:** the theory is that as people get older, their moral reasoning changes in six stages of moral development. Age-related moral reasoning develops alongside cognitive development irrespective of the culture in which a person grows up **Cognitive:** moral reasoning is a mental process	**Nature or nurture** Nature — because Kohlberg suggested changes in age cause changes in moral reasoning **Free will or determinism** Deterministic — age is the 'determiner' of changes in moral reasoning Disagrees with Freud's view that the superego is the 'moral part' of the personality **Situational or individual explanation** Individual — because the social situation should not affect moral behaviour
Lee et al. (1997) Evaluations of lying and truth telling	**Developmental:** a cross-cultural study which disagrees with Kohlberg and shows that moral thinking is affected by culture **Cognitive:** moral reasoning is a mental process **Social:** the cross-cultural study shows that social norms influence behaviour	**Nature or nurture** Nurture — because the study shows that moral reasoning is affected by culture

Biological psychology		
Sperry (1968) Split-brain study	**Biological:** it shows how different abilities are localised within the two hemispheres of the brain and how distinct areas of the brain control specific behaviours	**Nature or nurture** Nature — in right-handed people the left hemisphere controls language and if the left hemisphere is damaged language ability may be lost **Free will or determinism** Deterministic — damage to the left hemisphere will cause language loss **Psychology as a science** Scientific experimentation — looks at physical 'brains' rather than metaphysical 'minds'
Casey et al. (2011) Neural correlates of delay of gratification	**Biological:** the study uses longitudinal and correlational methods to suggest that there is a biological (neural) basis to self-regulation	**Nature or nurture** Nature — there is a biological basis for self-control **Free will or determinism** Deterministic — the ability for self-control' is an innate trait **Psychology as a science** Scientific explanation — but both longitudinal and correlational — should not make statements about cause and effect
Blakemore and Cooper (1970) Impact of early visual experience	**Biological:** an example of early and unethical research into brain plasticity, in which evidence suggests that the visual environment has an effect on cats' visual neurons	**Nature or nurture** Both (interactionist) — shows that the environment can have an effect on brain structure **Ethics** Breaks ethical guidelines regarding the use of non-human animals in psychological research
Maguire et al. (2000) Taxi drivers	**Biological:** a more up-to-date study demonstrating brain plasticity in humans using scientific techniques (MRI scans). The study shows that the biology of the brain is altered by experiences	**Nature or nurture** Both (interactionist) — because the hippocampi are important for memory and the environment can have an effect on the structure of the hippocampi

Individual differences		
Freud (1909) Little Hans	**Individual differences:** the longitudinal and qualitative case study of a single boy — it explains a way in which people may differ by developing a phobia **Developmental:** Freud suggests the development of the personality in five psychosexual stages **Psychodynamic:** Freud's theory of psychosexual development (especially the Oedipus complex) is used to explain little Hans' phobias and fantasies	**Psychology as science** Psychodynamic theories are unfalsifiable and unscientific **Situational or individual explanation** Individual — shows how individual personality is developed **Nature or nurture** Both — in Freud's theory, the id is our nature, but the ego and superego develop as a result of nurture **Free will or determinism** Deterministic — the past determines present behaviour
Baron-Cohen et al. (1997) Autism in adults	**Individual differences:** it explains how autistic traits (Asperger syndrome) affect how people behave **Cognitive:** the ability to recognise emotion in the eyes requires a mental process	**Situational or individual explanation** Individual — shows how individual traits affect behaviour
Gould (1982) A nation of morons: bias in IQ testing	**Individual differences:** it reviewed the development of tests to measure intelligence which is a way in which people differ	**Psychology as a science** Shows how difficult it is to avoid cultural bias in what are supposed to be objective IQ tests
Hancock et al. (2011) Language of psychopaths	**Individual differences:** it suggests that differences such as psychopathy can be measured **Psychodynamic:** uses concepts such as ego development and psychological 'distancing', and thrill-seeking drives, which 'sound' Freudian **Cognitive:** producing language is a cognitive process and this is a study of differences in how people use language	**Psychology as a science** Can textual analysis of qualitative data be regarded as 'science'? **Situational or individual explanation** Individual — suggests that murder is caused by individual traits not situational factors

You should be able to answer the following questions for each of the core studies.

Describe the research
- Outline the context and aim of the research.
- What research method and design was used?
- Describe how the participants were selected and who they were.
- If appropriate what was the independent variable (IV)? (There may be more than one.)
- What was the dependent variable (DV) and how was it operationalised?
- Describe the study procedure (i.e. what the participants were asked to do).
- Describe any controls that were used and explain why these were needed.
- Describe and explain the results.
- Outline the results (the data) of the research.
- Explain what the researchers concluded from the results.

Evaluate the study
- Evaluate the strengths and weaknesses of the research method and techniques.
- Evaluate the strengths and weaknesses of the type of data collected.
- Evaluate the ethical considerations.
- Consider the validity, reliability, any sampling bias and issues of ethnocentrism.
- Suggest how the study might be applied and explain how.
- Explain how the study relates to its area.
- Explain what the study informs us about one or more of the 'issues and debates'.

Questions & Answers

This section is not intended as a set of model answers to possible examination questions, or as an account of the right material to include in any examination question. It is intended simply to give you an idea of how your examination is structured and how you might improve your examination performance. You should read through the relevant topic in the Content Guidance before you attempt a question from the Question and Answers section. Look at the sample answers only after you have tackled the question yourself.

If you are studying AS psychology the exams are taken at the end of your 1-year course.

If you are studying A-level psychology the exams are all taken at the end of your 2-year course and the exams include synoptic questions to allow you to demonstrate your ability to draw together your skill, knowledge and understanding from across the full course and to provide extended responses.

AS Paper 2

Paper 2 will assess your knowledge and understanding of the ten core studies as well as your ability to evaluate the studies both on their own and in relation to the study they have been paired with. The core studies are placed within a broad area (approach) of investigation and within each area you are required to learn two core studies which are paired around key themes. For each key theme, you must learn both a classic and a contemporary study and taken as a group the studies represent a variety of research methodologies, designs, samples, sampling methods, issues and debates.

AS Paper 2 is assessed in a written 1 hour 30 minute exam in which 75 marks are awarded, comprising 50% of the AS. There are three sections in the exam, each carrying 25 marks, and you must answer *all the questions* in each of the three sections:
- Section A comprises short-answer questions on the core studies.
- Section B comprises questions on areas (approaches), perspectives and debates.
- Section C is the practical application section and in this section you are given a source and asked to apply your knowledge and understanding to psychological issues raised by the source.

A-level Paper 2

A-level Paper 2 is a **synoptic paper** and in your answers, as well as demonstrating knowledge and understanding of the core studies, areas, perspectives, issues and debates, you will be expected to refer to methodological issues such as:
- the strengths and weaknesses of the different research methods and techniques
- the strengths and weaknesses of different types of data
- ethical considerations
- validity
- reliability
- sampling bias
- ethnocentrism

This paper assesses your knowledge and understanding of the core studies as well as your ability to evaluate the studies, both on their own and in relation to the study they have been paired with. The core studies are placed within a broad area (approach) of investigation and within each area you are required to learn four core studies paired around key themes. For each key theme, you must learn both a classic and a contemporary study and taken as a group the studies represent a variety of research methodologies, designs, samples, sampling methods, issues and debates.

Paper 2 is assessed in a written 2-hour exam in which 105 marks are awarded, comprising 35% of the A-level. There are three sections in the exam, each carrying 35 marks, and you must answer *all the questions* in each of the three sections:

- Section A comprises short-answer questions on the core studies.
- Section B comprises questions on areas (approaches), perspectives and debates.
- Section C is the practical application section and in this section you are given a source and asked to apply your knowledge and understanding to psychological issues raised by the source.

Assessment objectives: AO1, AO2 and AO3 skills

Assessment objectives (AOs) are set by Ofqual and are the same across all A-level psychology specifications and all exam boards. The exams measure how students have achieved the following assessment objectives:

- **AO1:** Demonstrate knowledge and understanding of scientific ideas, processes, techniques and procedures.
- **AO2:** Apply knowledge and understanding of scientific ideas, processes, techniques and procedures in a theoretical context; in a practical context; when handling qualitative data and quantitative data.
- **AO3:** Analyse, interpret and evaluate scientific information, ideas and evidence, including in relation to issues, to make judgements and reach conclusions and to develop and refine practical design and procedures.

AO1 questions

Outline how biological psychology explains behaviour. (2 × AO1 marks)

AO1 + AO2 questions

Briefly outline one core study and **explain** how it could relate to [the person's] aggressive behaviour. (5 marks: 2 × AO1 marks + 3 × AO2 marks)

AO1 + AO3 questions

Discuss the extent to which psychology can be considered as a science. (12 marks: 3 × AO1 + 9 × AO3 marks)

Explain how any one core study can be considered to be located within the area of social psychology. Support your answer with evidence from appropriate psychological studies. (5 marks: 1 × AO1 + 4 × AO3 marks)

Identify and discuss four ethical considerations in relation to the study of individual differences. Support your answer with evidence from appropriate psychological studies. (20 marks: 4 × AO1 + 16 × AO3 marks)

Effective examination performance

Read the question carefully because marks are awarded only for the specific requirements of the question *as it is set*. Do not waste valuable time answering a question that you *wish* had been set.

Make a brief plan before you start writing an extended answer. There is space on the exam paper for planning and a plan can be as simple as a list of points, but you must know what, and how much, you plan to write. Time management in exams is vital.

Sometimes a question asks you to outline something. You should practise doing this in order to develop the skill of précis. Be aware of the difference between AO1, AO2 and AO3 commands (injunctions). You will lose marks if you treat AO3 commands such as 'discuss' as an opportunity to write more descriptive (AO1) content. Read the question command carefully and note the relevant skill requirement in your question plan.

Marks are awarded in **bands** for:

- **AO1:** the amount of relevant material presented, where low marks are awarded for brief or inappropriate material and high marks for accurate and detailed material.
- **AO2:** the level and effectiveness of application of psychological knowledge, where low marks are awarded for superficial consideration of a restricted range of issues and high marks for a good use of accurate and relevant material.
- **AO3:** the extent to which the answer demonstrates understanding by good analysis and interpretation and/or evaluation and argument that is relevant to the demands of the question.

Questions in this guide

This section comprises example AS and A-level questions.

AS questions: Section A — 5 questions; Section B — 5 questions; Section C — 5 questions

A-level questions: Section A — 5 questions; Section B — 4 questions; Section C — 4 questions

Note: A-level students should attempt all AS and A-level questions. AS students can attempt the Section B and Section C A-level questions but should use the AS core studies as the 'evidence' to support the answers.

The section is structured as follows:

- example question in the style of the exam
- example student response at grade A/B (Student A)
- example student response at grade C/D (Student B)

Exam comments

All student responses are followed by comments. These are preceded by the icon **ⓔ**. These comments may indicate where credit is due, strengths in the answer, areas for improvement, specific problems, common errors, lack of clarity, irrelevance, mistakes in meanings of terms and/or misinterpretation of the question. Comments may also indicate how example answers might be marked in an exam. Exam comments on the questions are preceded by the icon **ⓔ**. They offer tips on what you need to do to gain full marks.

■ AS exam-style questions

Section A: core studies

1 Describe two ways participants were deceived in Bocchiaro et al.'s study into disobedience and whistleblowing.

(4 marks)

e The question injunction is 'describe' so these are AO1 marks. You need to demonstrate your understanding of how the Bocchiaro et al. study deceived participants. You are not expected to provide more than 4 minutes of writing.

Student A

The participants were deceived because they were told that the experimenter was investigating the effects of sensory deprivation and that a recent experiment in Rome had harmed participants, some of whom had hallucinations, **a** but this was deception because no such experiment had taken place **b**.

Participants were deceived because they were told that they were writing a statement about the research into sensory deprivation that would be mailed to the list of students whose names they had given **c**, but this was untrue as the researchers were only interested in whether the participant blew the whistle or not **d**.

---

e **4/4 marks awarded.** Student A leaves nothing to chance and the description is accurate, thorough and coherent. In **a** and **b** one way the participants were deceived is identified and described accurately. In **c** and **d** a second way that participants were deceived is identified and described accurately. This is a thorough A-grade answer.

Student B

The participants were deceived because they were told that the experimenter was investigating the effects of sensory deprivation which was not true. **a**

Participants were deceived because they were told that a university ethics committee would be sent their feedback but this was not true. **b**

---

e **2/4 marks awarded.** In **a** and **b** Student B has very briefly identified sources of deception but has not described why these were 'deceptions'. This is a probable C/D-grade answer.

2 Bandura et al.'s study of transmission of aggression gathered quantitative data. Explain one advantage of gathering this type of data in this study.

(3 marks)

e The question injunction is 'explain' so these are AO3 marks. You need to demonstrate your understanding of how/why quantitative data were an advantage in the Bandura et al. study. You are not expected to provide more than 4 minutes of writing.

Student A

Gathering quantitative data is an advantage because it allows for comparisons to be made between groups of participants. 🅰 For example, it was easy to compare the amount of imitated and non-imitated aggression between girls and boys to see whether gender has an effect on imitated aggression, 🅱 and to compare whether there was any difference in the amount of aggression imitated in the same sex or opposite sex role model conditions to see whether the gender of a role model is important. 🅲

ⓔ **3/3 marks awarded.** In 🅰 to 🅲 the student gives an accurate, clear and fully contextualised suggestion as to why collecting quantitative data was an advantage to Bandura et al.

Student B

Gathering quantitative data is an advantage because it allowed for comparisons to be made between the amount of aggressive behaviour by girls and boys. 🅰

ⓔ **2/3 marks awarded.** In 🅰 the student gives an accurate and partially contextualised suggestion as to why collecting quantitative data is an advantage, but has not shown why being able to compare the aggression in girls and boys is actually a strength.

3 **Describe how the effect of the leading question was measured in the Loftus and Palmer study into eyewitness testimony.**

(4 marks)

ⓔ The question injunction is 'describe' so these are AO1 marks. You need to demonstrate your understanding of *how* Loftus and Palmer measured (operationalised) the effect of the leading question. You are not expected to provide more than 4 minutes of writing.

Student A

Student participants watched a video of a car accident and then each wrote an account of what they had seen. Then they were divided into five groups and each filled in a questionnaire which included the leading question: 'How fast were the cars going when they bumped/contacted/collided/hit/smashed each other?' 🅰 Each group had one of the five variations of the verb and differences in estimated speed were compared to see the effect of the leading question. 🅱 In experiment 2, student participants, in three groups of 50, were shown a film of a car accident and were given a questionnaire on which they estimated the speed of the car crash. Group 1 were asked the leading question containing the word 'hit', group 2 were asked it with the word 'smashed' and a control group was not asked a leading question. 🅲 A week later the participants returned and were asked: 'Did you see any broken glass?' The number of students who said that they had seen broken glass was taken as a measure of the effect of the leading question (hit or smashed) because there was no broken glass on the film. 🅳

ⓔ 4/4 marks awarded. In `a–d` the student gives a clear, accurate and explicit description of how the effect of the leading question was measured. The strength of this answer is that the student accurately describes the effect of the leading question as the operationalised DV in both experiment 1 and experiment 2.

Student B

Student participants watched a video of a car accident and were divided into five groups and each filled in a questionnaire which included the leading question: 'How fast were the cars going when they bumped/contacted/collided/hit/smashed each other?' `a` In experiment 2, participants were shown a film of a car accident and were given a questionnaire. One group was asked the leading question containing the word 'hit', group 2 were asked it with the word 'smashed' and a control group was not asked a leading question. A week later the participants returned and were asked: 'Did you see any broken glass?' `b`

ⓔ 2/4 marks awarded. In `a` the student gives an accurate description of the procedure, but has not explained how the effect of the leading question was measured. There is no mention of how the estimated speed was taken as a measure of the effect of the leading question. In `b` there is no mention of how the responses to the question about 'seeing broken glass' is taken as a measure of the effect of the leading question.

4 In the Chaney et al. 'Funhaler' study, describe the external influence on behaviour. (2 marks)

ⓔ The question injunction is 'describe' so these are AO1 marks. You need to demonstrate your understanding of how the Funhaler study is a study of external influence.

Student A

The external influence in the Chaney et al. 'Funhaler' study is the bell and the whistle attached to the inhaler that provides 'fun' to the child, and through the process of operant conditioning and positive reinforcement in which the child learns through consequences, the child is encouraged to continue to use the inhaler correctly.

ⓔ 2/2 marks awarded. The student gives a detailed, accurate and contextualised description of the external influence on behaviour.

Student B

The external influence in the Chaney 'Funhaler' study is the bell and the whistle attached to the inhaler that makes the inhaler more fun.

ⓔ 1/2 marks awarded. The student gives a partial answer, but misses the important point —'the external influence' is not the bell and whistle, but is the operant conditioning/positive reinforcement of behaviour.

5 Outline how social psychology explains behaviour. (2 marks)

e The question injunction is 'outline' so these are AO1 marks. You need to demonstrate your understanding of the assumptions of the social area in psychology.

Student A

Social psychologists assume that situational factors rather than individual characteristics influence behaviour, and that social interaction with other people, such as friends, family and peer groups, influences behaviour.

e **2/2 marks awarded.** The student has given an accurate outline of the assumptions of the social approach.

Student B

Social psychologists assume that other people have an effect on behaviour, for example Milgram showed that people follow orders given by those of high social status.

e **1/2 marks awarded.** The student gives a partial and rather vague answer. The example adds some credit but not enough for 2 marks. Compare this answer to the one given by Student A.

Section B: areas, perspectives and debates

6 a Outline how social psychologists explain behaviour. (2 marks)

e The question injunction is 'outline' so these are AO1 marks. You need to demonstrate your understanding of how social psychologists explain behaviour.

Student A

Social psychologists suggest that behaviour is influenced by the social situation people are in, by people around us, by peer groups and especially by people having power and high social status. **a**

---

e **2/2 marks awarded. a** The student gives a clear and accurate description.

Student B

Social psychologists suggest that behaviour is influenced by the social situation people are in. **a**

---

e **1/2 marks awarded. a** This is a vague and partial answer.

6 b Suggest one advantage of claiming that behaviour is due to the situation people are in. Support your answer from one appropriate core study. (3 marks)

e The question injunction is 'suggest one advantage' so these are AO3 marks. You need to demonstrate your understanding of an advantage of the social/situational approach. You are not expected to provide more than 3 minutes of writing.

Your answer could suggest that claiming that behaviour is due to the situation:

- has useful applications because it suggests that if we change the situation people are in we can change their behaviour
- allows us to study the behaviour of groups of people rather than individuals
- is a reductionist explanation for behaviour because it ignores the effect of biology and of individual differences on behaviour

---

Student A

One advantage of claiming that behaviour is due to situational factors, rather than to individual characteristics, is that it is useful because it helps us understand why, in some situations, people are influenced by others to behave in an anti-social manner. **a** For example, in his experiment looking at obedience Milgram found that 40 American men followed orders and gave potentially fatal electric shocks to a complete stranger who made a trivial 'word pair' mistake. Milgram explained that the obedience level was high because of the high social status of Yale University, and concluded that the participants had become 'agents' of the person giving the order, ceasing to take the responsibility for their own actions. **b** This and other social research is useful because it explains why otherwise 'good' people can be influenced by the situation they are in to behave badly. **c**

ⓔ 3/3 marks awarded. a–c The student has described a clear, detailed and contextualised advantage supported with appropriate evidence from Milgram. The strength of the answer is the last sentence c in which the student demonstrates a clear understanding of the application of social research.

> **Student B**
>
> One advantage of claiming that behaviour is due to situational factors is that it helps us understand why people behave in an anti-social manner. a For example, in an experiment at Yale University, Milgram found that American men followed orders and gave potentially fatal electric shocks to a complete stranger. b

ⓔ 1/3 marks awarded. In a the student makes a valid point, but b is a statement rather than an explanation/argument to support the point made.

6 c Suggest one disadvantage of claiming that behaviour is due to the situation people are in. Support your answer from one appropriate core study.   (3 marks)

ⓔ The question injunction is 'suggest one disadvantage' so these are AO3 marks. You need to demonstrate your understanding of a disadvantage of the social approach. You are not expected to provide more than 3 minutes of writing.

Your answer could suggest the following.

- It is a reductionist explanation as it ignores individual traits and biological factors which influence behaviour.
- It is often expensive to make appropriate environmental changes.
- Managing behaviour in one situation often leads to its displacement into another.

> **Student A**
>
> One disadvantage of claiming that behaviour is due to situational factors, rather than to individual characteristics, is that is that it is reductionist as it ignores biological factors as well as individual differences. a For example, in his study of obedience Milgram found that only 26 of the 40 American male participants administered the maximum electric shock of 450 volts. This demonstrates that the men were not all influenced in the same way by the social situation and that individual differences must also have been important. b This reductionism is a disadvantage because if we ignore factors such as biology and personality we may underestimate the extent to which people will respond differently in extreme social situations. c

ⓔ 3/3 marks awarded. In a to c the student has described a clear, detailed and contextualised disadvantage, supported with appropriate evidence from Milgram. The strength of the answer is that the student demonstrates a clear understanding of situational and dispositional explanations.

Student B

One disadvantage of claiming that behaviour is due to situational factors is that it is reductionist because it ignores cognitive and biological explanations for behaviour. **a** For example, Sperry found that only the left hemisphere of the brain is capable of language. **b**

e **1/3 marks awarded.** **a** The student makes a valid point, but **b** the point about Sperry is not relevant to the question.

6 d **Explain how one core study can be considered to be in the area of social psychology.** (5 marks)

e The question injunction is explain and for this question there are 1 × AO1 mark and 4 × AO3 marks.

For the AO1 mark, you need to demonstrate your understanding of the ethical issues through reference to an appropriate social study (e.g. Milgram or Bocchiaro et al.)

For the AO3 marks, you should make judgements and reach conclusions as to how the study relates to social psychology. For example, Milgram's study into obedience can be explained by the social approach, as the context of the situation impacted on behaviour.

Student A

The study of obedience by Milgram can be considered to be in the area of social psychology as the topic of research was obedience and obedience involves social influence. **a** Milgram suggests that the high social status of Yale University influenced the participants resulting in high levels of obedience which might not be found in less highly regarded social settings. **b** Milgram also suggests that because the authority figure wore a white lab coat participants obeyed because they believed him to be a trusted scientist who should be obeyed. **c** The study by Milgram is an example of social psychology because it looks at how both the social situation (Yale) and the social status of others (the experimenter) influence behaviour. **d**

e **5/5 marks awarded.** **a–d** The student has given a clear, detailed and contextualised answer, demonstrating good knowledge and understanding of one appropriate psychological study. The outline is accurate and there is relevant evaluation and discussion of how the psychological study can be considered to be located within the area of social psychology. A strength of the answer is **d** in which the student clearly argues why the Milgram study belongs in the social area.

Student B

The study of obedience by Milgram is in the area of social psychology as the topic of research was obedience and obedience involves social influence. a Milgram looked at how the social status of Yale influenced the participants to follow immoral orders. b

e **2/5 marks awarded.** In a the student makes a valid point, demonstrating knowledge of one appropriate psychological study. But b adds little to the answer as there is little discussion of how the psychological study can be considered to be located within the area of social psychology.

6 e Discuss ethical issues arising from the study of social psychology. Support your answer with evidence from the core studies. (12 marks)

e The question injunction is 'discuss' and for this question there are 3 × AO1 marks and 9 × AO3 marks. For the AO1 marks, you need to demonstrate your knowledge and understanding of the ethical issues involved in social psychology by referring to specific evidence from core studies (e.g. Milgram or Bocchiaro et al.).

To gain AO3 marks, you should make judgements, and analyse and interpret ethical issues and how they relate to social psychology. Discussion should be focused and expressed clearly and fluently with a clearly developed line of reasoning. Your answer should include research evidence as part of the discussion and must relate to the study of social psychology, so studies such as Milgram and Bocchiaro et al. are the most appropriate psychological research to be included.

Possible discussion points might be:

- informed consent
- protection of participants
- deception
- long-term psychological harm
- short-term psychological harm/stress
- debriefing
- the right to withdraw
- confidentiality

Student A

Compliance with the ethical guidelines challenges social researchers on many fronts: how to gain informed consent while at the same time avoiding demand characteristics, how to avoid deception, how to protect participants from both long-term and short-term psychological harm while being unable to predict how people will respond to research procedures, and how to make sure participants have the right to withdraw while making sure that a sample remains. a

Psychologists should always gain fully informed consent from their participants and participants should not be deceived about what they will be asked to do. b While studying social obedience, Milgram broke both these ethical guidelines because participants were told they were taking part in a study of memory and learning, and were led to believe that the electric shocks were real. c However, if Milgram had told his participants the truth about the experiment, either they would not have volunteered to participate, or if they had, he would have been measuring demand characteristics not 'obedience'. The challenge for social psychologists is how to manipulate and observe social behaviour while at the same time following the ethical guidelines, because whether the topic of research is pro-or anti-social behaviour, as soon as people are told the true purpose of the study they tend to behave as they think the researcher expects them to. d

Also, in ethical research, participants must be given the right to withdraw, e but Milgram's participants were prodded to remain even though they were trembling with distress. This is unethical, but to gain a valid measure of obedience it was necessary to put participants under pressure because no one would obey any order if told 'you can leave if you choose to'. It is important to note that Milgram had not predicted that any of his participants would in fact obey. f

Social psychologists must protect participants from harm and distress. g At the end of the study, Milgram thoroughly debriefed his participants who said they were happy to have taken part, but during the experiment they were seen 'shaking and trembling' showing how distressed they were. Milgram had not tested his participants to check they were healthy, and, since one participant had a 'seizure' this experiment could have seriously harmed someone. And, even if participants are not physically harmed, social psychologists need to make sure participants do not leave their research feeling worse about themselves than before. h Some psychologists argue that if you warn people they will be deceived and they still agree to participate, they have given their consent, but it is difficult to argue that prospective participants can give informed consent to the unknown. i

Another issue for social psychologists is whether to pay people to participate in research, and what type of payment should be offered. j Bocchiaro paid some participants money and some in university course credits but since the participants were university students this raises the issue as to whether the 'paid' participants truly felt they had the right to withdraw, or whether any of their behaviours during the study should be seen as anything other than the result of social influence. k

@ **12/12 marks awarded.** Student A has left nothing to chance. This is a very effective answer which demonstrates knowledge and understanding of a wide range of ethical issues related to social psychology. The answer is well focused and the ideas are expressed fluently and clearly. There is consistent use of psychological terminology and a well-developed line of reasoning. In a the student identifies some ethical issues arising in social psychology. In b–f through effective argument, the student links the ethical guidelines of informed consent, deception and right to withdraw clearly to social psychology and evidence from Milgram effectively supports the points made. In g–i the student makes appropriate and informed points about the need to protect participants from harm, showing understanding of the issues. In j–k the student discusses the issue of paying participants and links this with the right to withdraw, effectively choosing Bocchiaro et al. as an example.

This is a long answer and probably more than the average student can write in 12 minutes — a top-band answer should discuss three points supported by evidence from the core studies.

Student B

Social psychologists should gain fully informed consent from their participants and participants should not be deceived about what they will be asked to do. [a] Milgram broke both these ethical guidelines because participants were told they were taking part in a study of memory and learning, and that the electric shocks were real. [b]

Also, in ethical research, participants must be given the right to withdraw, [c] but Milgram's participants were prodded to remain even though they were trembling with stress and not allowed to withdraw. [d]

Also psychologists should protect participants from harm and distress. [e] In the Milgram experiment participants were seen 'shaking and trembling' showing how distressed they were, although when debriefed by Milgram his participants said they had been glad to participate. [f]

However, it is difficult for social psychologists to follow ethical guidelines while studying people in their everyday lives. [g]

ⓔ **5/12 marks awarded.** The answer is not very effective. It shows some understanding but discussion is limited. In [a-e] the answer correctly identifies ethical issues but only applied to Milgram and a top-band mark can only be awarded if the use of a named study is justified — in other words, the student needed to explain why Milgram is an example of social psychology. In [e-f] a further ethical issue is raised and related to Milgram. In [g] the student ends by making a statement that is not justified by evidence or explained.

Section C: practical applications

What is a stroke?

A stroke is an injury to the brain. The brain controls everything we do including everything we interpret and understand. A stroke can cause problems with communicating if there is damage to the parts of the brain responsible for language. These functions are controlled by the left side of the brain in most people. As the brain controls the opposite side of our body, many people who have communication problems after a stroke also have weakness or paralysis on the right side of their body.

Published by the Stroke association, June 2011: www.stroke.org.uk

7 a Explain why this article can be seen as relevant to biological psychology. (4 marks)

ⓔ The question injunction is 'explain' and there are 2 × AO1 marks and 2 × AO2 marks. You need to demonstrate your understanding of how social psychologists explain behaviour. For the AO1 marks, you should demonstrate knowledge and understanding of the biological approach. For the AO2 marks, you should apply your knowledge and understanding of the biological approach in the context of the source article.

Student A

The article is relevant to biological psychology because it says that 'the brain controls everything we do' and that behaviour such as communication is influenced by a specific part of the brain. The article says that the left side of the brain is responsible for language and that damage by a stroke to the left side of the brain will cause problems with language and paralysis on the right side of the body. In saying that, the article suggests a direct relationship between the biology of the brain and behaviour.

ⓔ **4/4 marks awarded.** The answer is very effective. It shows clear and accurate application of knowledge and understanding to explain why the article is relevant to biological psychology.

Student B

The article is relevant to biological psychology because it says the left side of the brain is responsible for language and for the right side of the body.

ⓔ **1–2/4 marks awarded.** This is a reasonable but very brief answer. It could be improved by explaining that the article suggests that there is a biological cause for behaviour.

7 b Briefly outline one core study and explain how it could relate to the above article. (5 marks)

ⓔ The question injunctions are 'outline' and 'explain' and there are 2 × AO1 marks and 3 × AO2 marks. For the AO1 marks, you need to demonstrate your understanding by outlining a study from the biological approach, probably Sperry or Casey et al. You should refer to the method and results of the study. For the AO2 marks, you need to apply your understanding of the core study explicitly to the source article and should quote from the source article.

Student A

The article is correct that damage to the left side of the brain causes communication problems and Sperry showed that if you are right-handed the left hemisphere controls language. a Sperry used split-brain patients to find out what happens when the two brain hemispheres cannot communicate. Sperry completed a series of experiments with split-brain patients. Participants covered one eye, looked at a point in the centre of a screen, and pictures were presented to the left or right visual field. b When pictures appeared in the right visual field, thus processed in the left hemisphere, the patient could describe them in speech and writing. If a picture was presented to the left visual field, thus processed in the right hemisphere, the patient reported seeing nothing. c Sperry concluded that the left hemisphere (in right-handed people) is specialised for speech and language. This relates to the article which states that 'a stroke can cause problems with communicating if there is damage to the parts of the brain responsible for language' and that 'these functions are controlled by the left side of the brain in most people'. d

e **5/5 marks awarded.** In a–d the student has accurately outlined the fine detail from the Sperry study demonstrating good knowledge and understanding. One strength of the answer is that in a and d the student has explained how the Sperry study is relevant to the article.

Student B

Sperry completed a series of experiments with split-brain patients and concluded that the left hemisphere (in right-handed people) is specialised for speech and language. a This agrees with the article which says people will have problems communicating if there is damage to the parts of the brain responsible for language. b

e **2/5 marks awarded.** a The outline of the study lacks any detail, but there is some indication that the student appreciates why the Sperry study can be linked to the article. The answer would be improved had the student included some of the procedures and findings from Sperry, and in b been more selective in the information included about the article.

7 **c** **Identify one psychological issue raised by the above article. Support your answer with evidence from the article.** (4 marks)

e The question injunction is 'identify' and you are expected to apply your knowledge to the article. There are 2 × AO1 marks awarded for the identification of an appropriate issue, and 2 × AO2 marks awarded for the application of this issue to the context of the article.

You could raise one of the following issues:

- the biology of the brain influences behaviour
- damage to a specific part of the brain can be linked to specific behaviours
- behaviour is determined for us by biology (nature not nurture)
- language ability depends on the left side of the brain
- the left side of the brain controls the right side of the body

Student A

One issue raised by the article is the extent to which behaviour such as speech and language is caused by the biology of the brain (nature) or whether behaviours such as language are learned (nurture). **a** If Sperry is right, and the left hemisphere of the brain is the only part of the brain that supports language, then as the article suggests if there is damage to the left hemisphere people will have difficulty communicating. **b** However, if the behaviourist theory, that language is learned by operant conditioning, is correct, then stroke patients who have damage to the left hemisphere should be able to relearn language. **c**

(e) 4/4 marks awarded. In **a–c** the student gives a clear and concise answer which identifies an appropriate issue from the source article and shows knowledge and understanding of how the issue can be related to the source article.

Student B

One issue raised by the article is whether language ability depends on the left side of the brain. **a** Sperry suggests that the right hemisphere has no language ability but participants were seen to blush when a rude word was being processed in the right hemisphere so the right hemisphere must have some understanding of language. **b**

(e) 3/4 marks awarded. **a, b** The student identifies an appropriate issue and gives evidence from Sperry which shows knowledge and understanding, but the issue is not contextualised explicitly to the source article.

7 d Use your psychological knowledge to suggest a training programme to manage the issue you have identified. (6 marks)

(e) The question injunction is 'use your psychological knowledge' which means apply your knowledge. There are 2 × AO1 marks and 4 × AO2 marks. For AO1 your psychological knowledge and ideas are likely to be demonstrated through reference to therapies for stroke patients. For AO2 marks you are expected to apply your knowledge and understanding in the context of the issue identified in question 7(c).

Answers are likely to refer to the following:

- based on the theory of brain plasticity, offer intensive therapy to recover brain function
- educate people as to how to recognise signs of stroke and what action to take

- carry out a brain scan to determine how much damage has been done, and where, to the brain
- design ways of communicating with brain-damaged patients
- carry out longitudinal research to see how much brain damage repairs after stroke
- offer behaviourist learning programmes to see if language can be relearned

Student A

The issue raised in question 7c was the extent to which behaviour such as speech and language can be relearned following a left hemisphere stroke. **a** Following the stroke the extent to which the patient has difficulty with language should be assessed. **b** Then a programme of speech therapy involving practical exercises such as the patient repeating words and sounds should be offered. **c** The speech therapist should speak clearly and act as a verbal role model (Bandura et al.). **d** The patient should be positively reinforced (rewarded) for each sign of progress. **e** To involve both the left and right hemispheres of the brain in language processing the patient should be asked to listen to and repeat words linked to strong emotions. **f** A record should be kept of the progress made so that the effectiveness of the therapy can be monitored. **g**

e 5/6 marks awarded. This is a top-band answer. The suggested training programme is clear and details have been included about how it could be implemented and developed. The understanding and application of psychological knowledge is good. In **a** the student starts by restating the issue raised in 7c — this is a good idea. In **b–e** the student demonstrates knowledge and understanding by giving a 'step by step' description of a training programme based on behaviourist principles. The suggestion made in **f** would have been stronger had some additional evidence been referenced, but **g** adds a good clear finish to the suggested programme.

Student B

The issue raised in question 7c is whether language ability depends on the left side of the brain. **a** If this is the case then hospital staff should be trained to recognise which side of the brain a stroke has damaged. **b** A study should be carried out in a stroke ward. Only right-handed patients should be selected because lateralisation of the brain differs in left-handed people (Sperry). Patients should be divided into two groups, those who have difficulty with language and those who do not. MRI scans of the brains of all patients should be done to identify which part of the brain is damaged. **c** If the results show that patients who have difficulty with language also have damage to the left side of the brain, but those who do not have difficulty with language do not have damage to the left side of the brain, then staff should be trained to assist patients with left hemisphere strokes to communicate using pictures and/or sign language. **d**

e 6/6 marks awarded. This is a top-band answer. The suggested training programme is clear and details have been included about how it could be implemented. The understanding and application of psychological knowledge is good. In **a** the student starts by restating the issue raised in 7c — this is a good idea. In **b-c** the student demonstrates knowledge and understanding (based on Sperry) by giving a 'step by step' description of the elements of a training programme. The point made in **d** adds a clear final suggestion to the programme.

7 e* Evaluate your suggested training programme. (6 marks)

* This is a synoptic question so you can refer to your learning from Component 1.

ⓔ The question injunction is 'evaluate' and there are 6 × AO3 marks. Evaluation may refer to:

- financial implications
- resources available
- cooperation between the agencies/individuals involved
- time constraints
- practical constraints
- ethics
- methodological points

Other appropriate points will also be credited.

For a top-band answer your evaluation will be relevant and appropriate details will be included. You should give more than one link to the training programme (described in your answer to 7d) and you should show understanding in the expression and use of psychological terminology and make clear and logically structured arguments.

Student A

A programme of speech therapy based on behaviourist learning principles was recommended. **a** Important ethical issues are raised by suggesting this behaviourist therapy for stroke patients. First, have the patients given informed consent? Because if they cannot communicate we cannot be sure they understand what is happening. Second, are the patients reminded that they can withdraw from the therapy, and if so do they understand their rights? **b** A practical issue is that if nurses are to be trained to deliver speech therapy on hospital wards how will they manage this as well as their nursing role? **c** A third issue is the cost arising from intensive behaviourist therapy. This therapy will take a long time and, as it is ongoing, will be costly. How will the therapy be funded? **d** Yet another issue arises from the need to monitor the programme of therapy. How will the effectiveness of the therapy be measured, over what period of time, and how will individual differences between patients be controlled? Also, it would be unethical to randomly allocate some patients to therapy and other patients to no therapy, but without a control group the effectiveness of the therapy cannot be scientifically tested. **e** Finally, the evidence for offering behaviourist speech therapy is weak, and Sperry's research clearly suggests that biology (nature) rather than learning (nurture) supports language ability. **f**

ⓔ 5–6/6 marks awarded. This is a top-band answer. The student leaves nothing to chance. The evaluation is clear and argued effectively. All the points made are relevant and are linked explicitly to the training programme. In **a** the student starts by restating the training programme described in 7d — this is a good idea. In **b–f** the student identifies and explains five evaluation points, each one demonstrating knowledge and understanding. The final points **e** and **f** add strength to the answer as they demonstrate synoptic understanding of scientific research methods and of the debate regarding nature vs nurture.

> ### Student B
>
> In 7d it was suggested that an experimental study should be carried out in a stroke ward and that staff should be trained to assist patients with left hemisphere strokes to communicate using pictures and/or sign language. **a** Ethical issues are raised by suggesting that staff communicate with some stroke patients using pictures and signs, because patients may find this type of communication embarrassing and they may be distressed at being treated differently from other patients. **b** Also the MRI scans will be expensive, as will be the staff training, adding to the cost of treating the patients. **c**

ⓔ 3/6 marks awarded. a, b The evaluation is reasonable and some details have been included to explain the implications. There are also links to the training programme. Understanding, expression and use of psychological terminology are clear, but in **c** the suggested issue is basic common sense and is not related to psychological knowledge.

■A-level exam-style questions

Section A: core studies

1 **Outline how Levine investigated helping behaviour in his study into cross-cultural altruism.** (4 marks)

ℯ The question injunction is 'outline' so these are AO1 marks. You need to demonstrate your knowledge and understanding of *how* Levine investigated helping behaviour. This is an outline so be brief but clear — you are not expected to provide more than 4 minutes of writing.

> **Student A**
>
> A field experiment was conducted in 23 large cities around the world. Three types of helping behaviour were measured: alerting a pedestrian who had dropped a pen; offering to help a pedestrian with a hurt leg trying to reach a pile of dropped magazines; assisting a blind person across the street. Opportunity samples of adults in each of the cities (e.g. Rome, Madrid) were approached in each of the three conditions and the frequency of help was measured.

ℯ **3/4 marks awarded.** This is a clear and accurate outline of how Levine investigated helping behaviour that includes reference to different locations, and the three IVs. The answer would be improved had the student included some information about the aim of the study. For example, *to investigate whether cultural norms influence helping behaviour* a field experiment was conducted in 23 large cities around the world.

> **Student B**
>
> A field experiment was conducted in different cities around the world. Opportunity samples of adults in each of the cities were approached to see who would help either a pedestrian who had dropped a pen or helping a blind person across the street.

ℯ **2/4 marks awarded.** This outline includes reference to the different locations and at least two of the IVs.

2 **Give one example of the results from the Simons and Chabris study of visual inattention and explain it in terms of visual inattention.** (4 marks)

ℯ The question injunctions are 'give one example' and 'explain'. There are 2 × AO1 marks and 2 × AO2 marks. For the AO1 marks, you need to outline one of the results from the Simons and Chabris study. For the AO2 marks, you need to explain what the results you have outlined tell us about visual inattention.

Student A

In the easy task condition, when watching the white team play and counting white team passes, only eight participants reported seeing the gorilla compared to 67 when watching the black team and counting black team passes. Participants who were watching the white team were so focused on the colour white that they were less likely to see the 'black' gorilla than when they were watching the black team. This suggests that when people are engaged in a task that requires them to pay close attention to one aspect of the environment (e.g. the colour white), visual inattention occurs when other large objects are not 'seen'.

e **4/4 marks awarded.** This is a clear and accurate outline of one of the results and a suitable explanation for why visual inattention occurs.

Student B

46% of participants did not see the unexpected object (either the umbrella woman or the gorilla).

e **2/4 marks awarded.** The marks awarded are the AO1 marks for the accurate outline of one result. No AO2 marks are awarded as the student has not given an explanation for the result.

3 **Describe one difference between the Blakemore and Cooper study of visual development and the Maguire et al. study of taxi drivers.** (3 marks)

e The question injunction is 'describe' so these are AO1 marks. You need to demonstrate your knowledge of one difference between these two studies. You could look at methodology, sampling, ethics, the area/approach, the type of data collected or any relevant point of difference.

Student A

One difference between the Blakemore study of visual development and the Maguire study of taxi drivers is the sample they used. Maguire's participants are the brain scans of human adult males, either taxi drivers or not, but Blakemore's participants are non-human animals (kittens).

e **3/3 marks awarded.** An appropriate difference is identified and described and supported with evidence from both the named studies.

Student B

One difference between the Blakemore study and the Maguire study of taxi drivers is ethics. Maguire followed all the BPS ethical guidelines; Blakemore is unethical.

🄔 **2/3 marks awarded.** An appropriate difference is identified and supported with evidence from one of the studies — Maguire et al. followed BPS guidelines. However, there is no contextualised explanation as to why Blakemore and Cooper is unethical.

4 Describe the purpose of the 'basic emotion recognition task' (emotion task) in the Baron-Cohen et al. study into autism in adults. (2 marks)

🄔 The question injunction is 'describe' so these are AO1 marks. Your answer needs to be a description *of why* the participants were tested with the basic emotion recognition task.

Student A

The basic emotion task was included as a control, so that Baron-Cohen could check whether, if the Asperger adults had poor scores on the eyes task, this could be explained by their inability to recognise basic facial expressions such as happiness, sadness and fear etc.

🄔 **2/2 marks awarded.** This is a clear, accurate and contextualised description, demonstrating a clear understanding of the purpose of the basic emotion task.

Student B

The basic emotion task was included to check whether the participants could recognise emotions shown on full faces.

🄔 **1/2 marks awarded.** This is a vague and partial answer and there is no contextualisation.

5 Suggest how the Hancock et al. study of the language of psychopaths is relevant to the area of individual differences. (3 marks)

🄔 The question injunction is 'suggest' and it implies that an explanation is required so these are AO3 marks. Your answer needs to give a brief outline of the individual differences area, then suggest why Hancock et al.'s study is relevant to this area and it must be supported with evidence from the study.

Student A

The individual differences area assumes that everyone is unique in their biological makeup, their personal qualities and their social experiences, and proposes that these differences are displayed through behaviour. 🄰 Hancock's study of psychopaths is relevant to this area because Hancock showed that the language used by psychopaths is different. According to Hancock, criminal psychopaths use more past tense verbs in their language and this shows how detached they are from their violent crimes. 🄑 However, because Hancock suggests that all psychopaths show these language differences, this difference seems to apply to a group of people rather than to an individual. 🄒

ⓔ 3/3 marks awarded. This is a top-band answer. It is a clear, accurate and contextualised suggestion. In ⓐ the student gives an accurate outline of the individual differences area. In ⓑ the student gives a contextualised explanation for why the Hancock et al. study is included in the individual differences area, and supports the explanation by evidence from the study. Then in ⓒ the student demonstrates knowledge and understanding by suggesting a thoughtful 'counter argument'.

The individual differences area assumes that everyone is different ⓐ and Hancock's study of psychopaths is relevant to this area because Hancock showed that the language used by psychopaths is different to the way most people use language. ⓑ

ⓔ 1/3 marks awarded. This is a vague and partial answer. In ⓐ the student gives an uninformed outline of the assumptions of the individual differences area. In ⓑ the answer is vague and no evidence from Hancock et al. is quoted in support. The word 'difference' is repeated and not expanded, evidenced or explained.

Section B: areas, perspectives and debates

6 a Describe the difference between a biological explanation for behaviour and a cognitive explanation for behaviour. (4 marks)

ℯ The question injunction is 'describe' so these are AO1 marks. You need to demonstrate your knowledge of the difference between biological and cognitive explanations for behaviour.

Student A

The biological explanation for behaviour suggests that objective physical facts such as brain structures, genes or hormones are the cause of behaviour. ⓐ On the other hand, the cognitive explanation suggests that metaphysical mental processes such as memory and attention are the cause of behaviour. ⓑ

ℯ **4/4 marks awarded.** The description of the difference is detailed and accurate. In ⓐ the student accurately describes the assumptions of the biological approach and in ⓑ the student accurately describes the assumptions of the cognitive approach.

Student B

The biological explanation for behaviour suggests that the biology of the brain causes behaviour. On the other hand, the cognitive explanation suggests that the mind causes behaviour.

ℯ **1/4 marks awarded.** Student B has given a very basic description which for the biological approach lacks accuracy and for the cognitive approach is too sparse.

6 b Explain how one psychological study can be considered as providing a cognitive explanation for behaviour. (5 marks)

ℯ The question injunction is 'explain'. There are 1 × AO1 mark and 4 × AO3 marks. For the AO1 mark, you should give a brief outline of any appropriate study from the cognitive area and for a top-band mark the named study must be justified. For the AO3 marks, you should interpret and evaluate the study in order to explain why and how it provides a cognitive explanation for behaviour.

Student A

Grant et al. carried out a study of cognitive psychology to find out whether we remember information we have learned better in the context in which we learned it. ⓐ In this laboratory experiment, participants were divided into four conditions — either learn in silence and recall in silence, learn in silence and recall in noise, learn in noise and recall in noise, or learn in noise but recall in silence. ⓑ

The participants read a 2-page article on psychoimmunology and were then tested. The recall scores were higher when the learning and recall were undertaken in the matching (noise or silence) environment. ⓒ This provides a cognitive explanation for behaviour because the topic of the research is memory which is a hidden mental process, ⓓ and the research shows how environmental factors can affect mental (cognitive) processes of learning and remembering. ⓔ

ⓔ **5/5 marks awarded.** In `a–c` the answer shows accurate knowledge and understanding of the aims, procedures and findings of the Grant et al. study which is an appropriate psychological study. In `d` and `e` there are two ways that the study provides a cognitive explanation for behaviour.

Student B

Simons and Chabris carried out a study of cognitive psychology because they carried out a study of attention and why we sometimes do not notice objects. Their participants watched a video of a basketball team playing and were asked to count the passes. Most of the participants did not notice a gorilla walk across the game. `a` This is a cognitive study because attention is a mental process. `b`

ⓔ **2/5 marks awarded.** In `a` the outline is brief and not wholly accurate. In `b` the final sentence is a statement rather than an explanation and there is little evaluation of how the psychological study provides a cognitive explanation for behaviour.

6 c Evaluate the usefulness of providing a cognitive explanation for behaviour.
   Support your answer with evidence from one appropriate psychological study.   (6 marks)

ⓔ The question injunction is 'evaluate'. There are 1 × AO1 mark and 5 × AO3 marks. You will be awarded the AO1 mark for knowledge and understanding by stating what the cognitive explanation is. For the AO3 marks you must interpret, evaluate, make judgements and reach conclusions about the usefulness of the cognitive explanation. For a top-band mark you should refer to *more than one* strength *and* one weakness OR *more than one* weakness *and* one strength of a cognitive explanation, *all* supported by appropriate evidence from a psychological study. This is a lot to do for 6 marks.

Strengths of a cognitive explanation:

- It is useful because it suggests people have free will to choose how to behave.
- It uses experimental methods to reveal hidden mental processes.
- It suggests that people can change the way they think and thus change the way they behave.

Weaknesses of using a cognitive explanation:

- It is reductionist as it ignores biological and social individual factors which influence behaviour.
- It is difficult to reveal mental processes other than in laboratory experiments.

Student A

Research from the cognitive area is useful because it increases our understanding of mental processes such as memory and attention. For example, the Loftus and Palmer study of eyewitness memory demonstrated how, by asking witnesses leading questions, a false memory could be created. Research into memory has been useful as we now know that eyewitness memory may not be accurate. `a`

Another advantage of cognitive psychology is that it takes a scientific approach, and usually uses laboratory experiments to reveal mental processes. This means that cognitive research is especially useful because findings are valid and reliable. For example, Loftus and Palmer carried out their research using standardised procedures and high levels of control. In their research, all participants watched the films in the same environment, were asked the same questions about speed, so they could conclude that only the variation in the leading question caused the differences in estimated speed. b However, it is important to remember that mental processes can only be inferred and biological psychologists would argue that to understand human behaviour psychologists should study the physical brain rather than the metaphysical mind. c

A limitation of cognitive psychology is that it is reductionist to assume that mental thought processes are the only cause of behaviour. Although Loftus and Palmer looked at the mental processes involved in memory, biological psychologistsed, such as Maguire have shown that the physiology of the brain also influences memory and research by Grant et al. shows us that whether we recall something or not may depend on the situation in which we try to remember. d

e **6/6 marks awarded.** The student has referred to two strengths and one weakness supported by appropriate evidence from the Loftus and Palmer study. The answer shows good knowledge and understanding of the cognitive explanation as well as clear and accurate evaluation of its usefulness.

In a the student explains the usefulness of cognitive research accurately supported by evidence from Loftus and Palmer.

In b the student explains a second advantage of cognitive research by referring to scientific methodology, supported by evidence from Loftus and Palmer. This paragraph is strengthened by the clearly explained point c.

In the third paragraph, d the student presents reductionism as a clearly argued counter argument, again evidenced by knowledge from the core studies.

Student B

Research from the cognitive area is useful, for example the Loftus and Palmer study demonstrated how leading questions affect memory and that eyewitness memory is not reliable. a

Another advantage of cognitive psychology is that it uses laboratory experiments. For example, Loftus and Palmer carried out their two laboratory experiments so they could conclude that only the leading question caused the differences in estimated speed. b

A limitation of cognitive psychology is that it is reductionist because it ignores the biological and social influences that also affect behaviour so we cannot assume that mental thought processes are the only cause of behaviour. c

ⓔ 3/6 marks awarded. The student has referred to two strengths and one weakness, but there is little detail in the supporting evidence from the Loftus and Palmer study. The answer shows some knowledge and understanding of the strengths and limitations of the cognitive explanation.

In **a** the student gives a brief explanation of the usefulness of cognitive research, accurately supported by evidence from Loftus and palmer In **b** the argument is weak and 'list like', lacking in explanation. In **c** the point about reductionism is accurate, but support by evidence would add strength to the argument.

Hint: compare this answer with the one from Student A.

6 d* Cognitive psychologists often conduct research using laboratory experiments. Discuss the contribution that cognitive psychologists make to the assumption that psychology is a science.

(20 marks)

* This is a synoptic question. You may refer to any psychology you have learned in Component 1 or Component 2.

ⓔ The question injunction is 'discuss' and there are 4 × AO1 marks and 16 × AO3 marks. You are awarded AO1 marks for knowledge and understanding of the cognitive research. You achieve AO3 marks for interpreting, evaluating, making judgements and reaching conclusions about how the cognitive approach contributes to the argument that 'psychology is a science'. For a top-band mark you should make four points *all* supported by appropriate evidence from a psychological study.

Note: make a plan before you start to write and allow 20 minutes for your answer.

You need to demonstrate your knowledge and understanding of research methods (how science works) and you could:

- identify and describe features of the experimental method
- describe how the IV is isolated and manipulated
- describe ways by which the DV is operationalised and measured
- refer to the advantages and disadvantages of collecting quantitative data
- refer to the control of extra variables
- refer to the realism of the procedures
- refer to your knowledge of laboratory experiments in cognitive psychology
- refer to the strengths and limitations of laboratory-based experiments
- refer to a counter argument about the metaphysical nature of the mind

> ### Student A
>
> Some features are common in scientific research. Scientific researchers write testable, falsifiable hypotheses. They use experimental methods and try to control all variables except the independent variable (IV) which they manipulate. The research takes a quantitative, rather than qualitative, measure of the effect of the IV on the DV. In experimental methods, researchers use standardised procedures and use control groups to increase the validity and reliability of results. **a**

As suggested in the question, cognitive psychologists use experimental methods to study the hidden mental processes underlying memory and attention. For example, in the Loftus and Palmer second experiment, the use of a control group allowed the researchers to be sure that it was the use of the word 'smashed' that caused more participants to report seeing broken glass that was not present on the film. By the use of experimental methods Loftus and Palmer showed how a false memory could be created and how a scientific study of memory could be useful. b

Another cognitive study using scientific methods is Simons and Chabris who used controlled laboratory experiments to demonstrate how and why people who are paying close attention to a task, do not notice large objects nearby. After they had participated, participants who were counting the passes by the white team were astonished to see that they had not seen the gorilla. c By the use of replicable scientific methods, research by these cognitive psychologists has increased our understanding of human behaviour and contributed to the assumption that psychology is a science. d

However, scientific research using experimental methods often has low external validity because the procedures used in a laboratory may not measure how people behave in their everyday lives. For example, in experimental research into how memory is affected by context (Grant et al.) participants were asked to read and remember information about psychoimmunology, but people do not often have to remember information having no relevance to their interests in their everyday lives. e

It could be argued that, even though cognitive psychologists have contributed to psychology as science, it would be an advantage if they used less scientific methodologies, such as observation and self report, to gather subjective and qualitative evidence regarding human thought processes. Finally, it could be argued that the cognitive study of mental processes cannot be a science because minds are hypothetical and metaphysical, and that if psychology is to be recognised as a science, psychologists should study physical things like brains rather than minds. f

e **16–20/20 marks awarded.** Student A gives a highly effective answer. The well-focused discussion demonstrates understanding and analysis and the ideas are well structured and elaborated. There is consistent use of accurate psychological terminology and a developed line of reasoning. The evidence selected is appropriate to support the points made.

In a, the student provides an accurate description of the main characteristics of scientific research. In b, to demonstrate understanding and relevance, the student quotes Loftus and Palmer as an accurate example of scientific research. In c the student selects another example of scientific research in cognitive psychology and ends the paragraph d by referring back to the question of cognitive research as a contribution to science. In e the student presents a well-argued counter argument to discuss whether scientific methods reveal how people think in everyday life, and supports the argument with evidence from Grant et al. Finally, in f the student presents an argument suggesting that cognitive research cannot be scientific if it studies 'minds', demonstrating an understanding of the assumptions of science and of psychology. The strength of this answer is the clarity and coherence of the discussion. This is a probable A-grade answer.

Student B

Cognitive psychologists use experimental methods to study mental processes. Laboratory experiments are scientific and Loftus and Palmer used laboratory experiments to study eyewitness memory and found that it was not reliable. In their experiment Loftus and Palmer asked students to watch a video of a car accident and then gave them a questionnaire which included the leading question 'How fast were the cars going when they "contacted/hit/bumped/collided/smashed" each other?' The participants who were asked the question 'smashed' reported a higher speed. This research collected quantitative data so is scientific. [a]

Simons and Chabris also used laboratory experiments to research attention and why people may not notice large objects nearby. These research studies are scientific because controlled laboratory experiments are valid and reliable. [b]

However, being scientific can be a disadvantage because experimental research has low external validity when the procedures used in a laboratory are not like everyday life. For example, Moray played different messages to each ear of his participants but this would not happen in everyday life, so even though cognitive research is scientific is it not very useful. [c]

Some would argue that psychology is not a science anyway because methods such as self-report or case studies gather subjective qualitative data. But people may not reveal their true thought processes in self-report methods so laboratory experiments are a more valid way to study the mind. [d]

[e] **7–8/20 marks awarded.** This answer lacks focus and the expression of ideas in it lacks clarity, but there is some use of accurate psychological terminology and some evidence selected is appropriate to support the points made.

In [a], the student makes the mistake of describing too much AO1 evidence and the argument is rather 'circular', saying that laboratory experiments are scientific and thus Loftus and palmer is scientific but without referring to any of the characteristics of scientific research. The paragraph is not very focused on the question. [b] This is a statement rather than an explanation of why experimental methods are valid and reliable. In [c] the student argues that scientific research is not always an advantage, but does not relate this closely to the question about the contribution of cognitive research to 'psychology as a science'. In the final paragraph, [d] the argument about methodology could have been much more closely related to the question.

Section C: practical applications

In China, no one will help you after an accident

A recent video of a two-year-old getting hit by a van has stirred up Chinese attention.

The news clip shows a girl in Guangdong being run over by a van, and then 18 onlookers passing by without stopping or calling for help. The clip has revived the debate on whether bystanders should help accident victims.

The Chinese courts set a precedent in 2006 when a young adult trying to help an elderly woman who fell was sued for $6,076. According to Bloomberg, two separate polls in China determined that the majority of bystanders would not help an accident victim.

Since then, the issue of whether or not bystanders should help victims has been under heated debate. And many victims have not received potentially life-saving help for fear of lawsuits.

Based on an article by Andrew Chen, 17 October 2011, *Business Insider*: www.tinyurl.com/qjabd4r

7 a Identify one psychological issue raised by the above article. Support your
 answer with evidence from the article. (5 marks)

ⓔ The question injunction is 'identify' and the question infers that an explanation is also needed. There are 2 × AO1 marks and 3 × AO2 marks. For the AO1 marks, you need to demonstrate your understanding by outlining a study from the social approach, probably the Piliavin et al. study of helping or the Levine cross-cultural study of helping. You should refer to the method and results of the study. For the AO2 marks, you need to apply your understanding of the core study explicitly to the source article and should quote from the source article.

You might suggest:

- the behaviour of the people who do not help can be explained by the two-factor model of helping
- no one helps because of diffusion of responsibility

Or ask:

- Does fear of possible costs prevent us from helping strangers?
- Do bystanders help in countries other than China?
- What factors motivate people to help strangers in distress?

Student A

One issue raised by the above article is whether fear of possible costs does prevent us from helping strangers. The article suggests that 18 bystanders did not help the child because they feared being sued as 'a young adult trying to help an elderly woman who fell was sued for $6,076'. Following an experimental investigation into helping behaviour, Piliavin et al. concluded that two factors may explain why we do or do not help strangers in distress — empathy and self-interest. Piliavin suggests that an emergency situation creates empathic arousal in a bystander and that this arousal can be reduced by helping or by walking away. Piliavin also concluded that before we help we calculate and balance the possible cost of helping against the possible benefit of helping and that if we believe the costs are greater than the reward we will not help. This seems to suggest the article is correct and people did not help because of fear of legal costs.

ⓔ **5/5 marks awarded.** The answer shows accurate application of knowledge and understanding to identify an appropriate issue and this is supported by evidence from the article.

Student B

One issue raised by the above article is whether diffusion of responsibility explains why people did not help. The article mentions a girl in Guangdong being run over by a van, and then 18 onlookers passing by without stopping or calling for help'. Years ago, in a similar situation a young woman called Kitty Genovese was fatally stabbed in New York and there were 38 witnesses who did not help. Psychologists suggested diffusion of responsibility explains why no one helped — that when there are many potential helpers, no one helps because everyone thinks someone else will do it, thus no one takes the responsibility to help and no help is given.

ⓔ 4/5 marks awarded. The answer shows good application of knowledge and understanding to identify an appropriate issue and this is supported by evidence from the article. A final sentence to relate diffusion of responsibility back to the article would have improved the answer. The article says there were 18 onlookers, and had there not been so many diffusion of responsibility would have been less likely and someone might have helped.

7 b **Briefly outline one piece of psychological research and explain how it could relate to the issue you have identified in the above article.**
(8 marks)

ⓔ The question injunctions are 'outline' and 'explain' and there are 4 × AO1 marks and 4 × AO2 marks. For the AO1 marks you need to demonstrate your understanding by outlining a study that clearly relates to the issue you raised, probably Piliavin et al. or Levene. You should refer to the method and results of the study. For the AO2 marks, you need to apply your understanding of the core study explicitly to the issue raised by the source article and you should quote from the source article.

> ## Student A
>
> The issue raised is whether fear of possible costs prevents us from helping strangers. [a]
>
> Piliavin et al. carried out a field experiment to find out what motivates us to help strangers. The participants were an opportunity sample of passengers who happened to be on a New York subway train. On average there were 43 passengers in each trial. 70 seconds after the train left the station the male victim (black or white) staggered and collapsed (carrying either a cane or a bottle of alcohol). There were four victim conditions: white lame, black lame, white drunk and black drunk. Two female observers recorded how long it took for passengers to help as well as the race, gender and location of those who offered help. Piliavin found that 80% of first helpers were male, that the cane victim received spontaneous help 95% of the time but the drunk victim only 50% of the time and that 91% of the cane victims were helped before the role-model stepped in compared to only 24% of drunk victims. [b]
>
> Piliavin et al. concluded that two factors explain why we do or do not help strangers in distress — empathy and self-interest. Piliavin suggests that (i) an emergency situation creates empathic arousal in a bystander and that this arousal can be reduced by helping or by walking away, and that (ii) before we help we calculate the possible cost of helping against the possible benefit of helping and that if we believe the costs are greater than the reward we will not help. [c] So does fear of possible costs prevent us from helping strangers? Piliavin would argue that only if the possible costs are greater than the possible reward for helping, which in the case of the article is likely as the parents of the Chinese child who was run over are unlikely to be wealthy. [d]

(e) **8/8 marks awarded.** The outline is accurate and detailed. The student has justified the use of the named study and shows good understanding of why the study can be related to the identified issue in the article. Detailed reference is made to the main components of the study — the aim, research method, sample, procedures, findings and conclusions. There is a well-developed line of reasoning which is clear and logically structured. The information presented is relevant and substantiated.

In [a] the student restates the issue, which is a good idea. In [b] the outline given is clear, detailed and accurate. In [c] the conclusions of the study are thorough and in [d] these are related explicitly to the issue identified in the article.

Student B

The issue raised is whether diffusion of responsibility explains why people did not help. **a** Piliavin et al. carried out research to find out whether diffusion of responsibility prevented people from helping on the New York subway. Piliavin found that many people helped and there was no diffusion of responsibility. He concluded that two factors explain why we do or do not help strangers in distress — empathy and self-interest. Piliavin suggests that when we see an emergency situation this creates empathic arousal and that this arousal can be reduced by helping or by walking away. Also, before we help we calculate the possible cost of helping against the possible benefit of helping and if we believe the costs are greater than the reward we will not help. **b** If Piliavin is right we can conclude that even though in the article there were 18 bystanders, it was the perceived cost of helping, not diffusion of responsibility, that prevented onlookers helping. **c**

e **5–6/8 marks awarded.** The student has justified the use of the named study and shows good understanding of why the study can be related to the identified issue in the article, but the outline given lacks detail — details are missing, for example, research method, sample, procedures and findings. However, there is a developed line of reasoning which is logically structured and the information presented is relevant and justified.

In **a** the student restates the issue, which is a good idea. In **b** the outline lacks detail, but in **c** the conclusions of the study are related explicitly to the issue identified in the article.

7 c* Use your psychological knowledge to suggest how the issue you identified in question 7a could be managed.

(8 marks)

* This is a synoptic question.

e The question injunction is 'suggest' and infers that you must apply your psychological knowledge. There are 2 × AO1 marks and 6 × AO2 marks. You will gain AO1 marks for knowledge and understanding by referring to psychological theories and for showing how these could be developed to manage the issue identified. Answers are likely to refer to encouraging people to help others.

For the AO2 marks you could suggest:

- having the government offer rewards for people who help
- using role models on television to show people helping and being rewarded
- schools should include class sessions in which helping strangers is modelled and rewarded
- television could show a documentary of a person being helped and the helper being rewarded
- drivers who stop to help in an accident could be rewarded by cheaper car insurance

Your suggestions must be clear and details must be included about how they could be implemented and developed.

Questions & Answers

The issue raised in question 7a was whether fear of possible costs prevents us from helping strangers. The article implies that 18 bystanders did not help the child because they feared being sued and Piliavin suggests that people will be less likely to help if they believe the cost of helping is greater than the reward for helping. **a** If this is the case, then to encourage more people to help others in distress we need to bring about a situation in which people believe they will be rewarded for helping others. **b** Based on behaviourist learning theory, using operant conditioning, a programme could be developed to encourage those who help in emergency situations to believe they will receive a reward. **c** For example, the Chinese government could give financial rewards to anyone who is identified as having helped a stranger. **d** Also, based on social learning theory (Bandura), television programmes could show those who have helped being presented with their rewards, so those watching will learn to imitate the helping behaviour. **e** Finally, to encourage young children to grow up to help others, Chinese schools should organise classes in which young children watch adult role models helping strangers and being rewarded. **f** Bandura argues that young children observe adult behaviour and, especially if the behaviour is rewarded (positive reinforcement), that they will imitate the behaviour when they are older. **g**

e 7–8/8 marks awarded. The suggestions are clear and details have been included about how they could be implemented and developed. Understanding and application of psychological knowledge is good. There is a well-developed line of reasoning which is clear and logically structured. The information presented is relevant and substantiated.

In **a** the student restates the issue, which is a good idea. In **b** and **c** the student gives a justification for the suggestions that follow. In **d–g** the student makes three clear suggestions, based on behaviourist learning theories, which are sensible and relevant to the issue raised and to the article.

If fear of possible costs prevents us from helping strangers a programme should be developed to encourage those who help in emergency situations to believe they will receive a reward. **a**

For example, the Chinese government could give financial rewards to anyone who is identified as having helped a stranger. **b** Also, to encourage young children to grow up to help others, Chinese schools should organise classes in which children watch adult role models helping strangers and being rewarded so that they will imitate the behaviour when they are older. **c**

e 4/8 marks awarded. The suggestions are clear and some details have been included about how they could be implemented and developed, but the information is supported by limited psychological evidence — the knowledge is implied rather than explicit. The answer could be improved by including more details about the psychological theories/evidence on which the suggestions are based.

Note: compare this answer with the answer from Student A.

7 d* Evaluate how you would manage the issue you identified in question 7a. (14 marks)

* This is a synoptic question.

(e) The question injunction is 'evaluate' and there are 2 × AO2 marks and 12 × AO3 marks. For the AO2 marks you gain credit if you apply your knowledge and understanding of psychology to the suggestions you made for managing 'the issue'. For the AO3 marks you gain credit if the analysis and evaluation are appropriate and details are included. AO3 evaluation might refer to:

- funding the suggestion(s)
- resourcing the suggestion(s)
- ethics
- measuring the effectiveness of the suggestion(s)
- time and travel constraints
- methodological points

Other appropriate points will be credited.

Student A

To encourage people to help others in distress a programme based on behaviourist learning theory is to be developed to encourage those who help in emergency situations to believe they will receive a reward.

The first suggestion is that the Chinese government should give financial rewards to anyone who is identified as having helped a stranger. [a] This is not very practical as the government will have to define what sort of 'help' deserves reward and the programme may become very expensive for the Chinese government as many thousands of people will claim rewards for helping. Levine found that Shanghai was ranked 8th out of 23 cities for helping behaviour, which suggests that the Chinese people are more helpful to strangers than the article suggests. [b] Also, if claims for rewards are based on self-report it will be difficult to know whether a claim is genuine or not. [c] The second suggestion was that TV could show those who have helped being presented with their rewards, so those watching will learn to imitate the helping behaviour. [d] However, this would require the consent of the helpers, and many helpful Chinese people would prefer to remain anonymous and would not wish to appear on TV. [e] A third suggestion was that Chinese schools should organise classes in which young children watch adult role models helping strangers and being rewarded. [f] However, parental consent would be needed if children under 16 were to be involved in this 'experiment'. [g] In addition, there are many millions of Chinese children and it would be difficult to ensure that the role-modelled helping was carried out in the same way in all classes. [h] Also, the Bandura study of social learning measured the effect on the children's aggression immediately, but did not measure any long-term effect, so we could never be sure that, if years later the rate of helping in China did increase, this was caused by the role model classes. [i] Another reason why none of these suggestions may increase helping is that according to Piliavin, an important factor that motivates helping is empathy. [j] Thus, if potential helpers do not experience empathic arousal they will be unlikely to help even if they believe they will be rewarded for helping. [k]

ⓔ 13–14/14 marks awarded. Student A has left nothing to chance. The analysis and evaluation are clear and thorough, and many details have been included to explain the implications. There is a well-developed line of reasoning and evaluation points are based on psychological knowledge and understanding.

Points **a–c** are especially strong, and the evidence from Levine adds value to the point about the cost of rewarding helpers. Points **d–e** show understanding of practical issues, suggestions are clear and some details have been included. Points **f–i** are well argued and demonstrate understanding of the ethical guidelines and of methodological issues applied to the suggestion.

Finally, in points **j–k** the student argues a very strong point, explicitly based on knowledge of research, about the probable limitation of the suggestions. This is a well-written answer which is clear and logically structured. It is an A-grade answer.

Student B

The suggestion that the Chinese government should give financial rewards to anyone who is identified as having helped a stranger will be very expensive as there are millions of people in China and thousands may claim rewards for helping. **a** Also, if claims for rewards are based on self-report it will be difficult to know whether a claim is genuine or not. **b** The second suggestion that TV could show those who have helped being presented with their rewards is not very practical as we cannot be sure how many people will watch and we will not be able to measure the effect of the TV programme on rates of helping. **c** A third suggestion was young children should watch adult role models helping strangers and being rewarded, but parental consent would be needed if children under 16 were to be involved in this 'experiment'. **d** Also, the Bandura study of role modelling involved imitation of anti-social behaviour, and we cannot be sure children will imitate pro-social behaviour in the same way. **e**

ⓔ 7/14 marks awarded. Student B has written a reasonable evaluation with limited analysis and limited application of psychological knowledge. There are some details but the explanation and argument could have been improved.

Point **a** is a practical point but is not based on psychological evidence. Point **b** shows understanding of methodology but could have been explained further. Point **c** about not being able to measure the effect of the TV programme adds some value. Points **d–e** add some value as both points are relevant and based on psychological knowledge. Overall, this is a probable C/D-grade answer.

Knowledge check answers

1 The participants were deceived because they were told the electric shocks were real but they were not; they were deceived because they were told Mr Wallace was another participant but he was a stooge; they believed they could have been the learner but the 'drawing of straws' was fixed; they were deceived because they were led to believe it was the learning by Mr Wallace which was 'of interest' but it was their obedience that was being studied.

2 The participants were deceived because the cover story they were told about the effects of the sensory deprivation experiment was not true. They were also deceived because they were told that their statements would be sent to the students they had named in the mail, but this was not going to happen.

3 This was an opportunity sample because Piliavin had no control over who got on the train and participated — the sample were the passengers who just happened to be on the subway at 59th or 125th Street on the day(s) the study took place.

4 Diffusion of responsibility occurs when there are many potential helpers present at an emergency situation, and no one helps because everyone thinks that someone else will help so no one takes the responsibility for helping.

5 Simpatico cultures are defined as cultures in which there is pro-active concern with the social wellbeing of others.

6 A field experiment was conducted in 23 cities around the world. One neatly dressed individual appeared to require help. Three types of helping behaviour were measured: alerting a pedestrian who had dropped a pen, offering to help a pedestrian with a hurt leg trying to reach dropped magazines, assisting a blind person to cross the street.

7 The sample in experiment 1 was 45 university students allocated to five groups of nine. The sample in experiment 2 was 150 university students, allocated to two experimental groups of 50 and a control group of 50. The samples may be biased because university students are generally younger than the average age in the population, and age is also a factor that may affect the memory of an eyewitness.

8 The use of a control group in experiment 2, in which participants were not asked any questions about the speed of the crash, increased experimental validity, because Loftus and Palmer could then be sure that it was the different verbs used, 'hit' or 'smashed', that affected the responses to the question about 'seeing broken glass'.

9 Participants were allocated to one of four conditions: learn in silence, recall in silence; learn in silence, recall in noise; learn in noise, recall in noise; learn in noise, recall in silence. They wore headphones and either hearing noise or in silence read a 2-page article on psychoimmunology having been told they would be tested.

10 In the first experiment, in the non-attended message, a short list of simple words was played repeatedly (35 times) into one ear while at the same time a message was played to the other ear (the attended message) which the participant repeated as it was played (shadowed). After 30 seconds the participant was asked to recall the words presented in the non-attended message.

11 When watching the white team only 8 participants reported seeing the gorilla compared to 67 when watching the black team. Overall, 46% did not notice either the gorilla or the umbrella woman. Simons et al. explain that this happens because of visual inattention, and that visual inattention happens if people are already engaged in a task that requires attention (such as watching a videotape of a basketball game and counting passes) so they do not notice an unexpected event such as a gorilla walking across the screen.

12 According to Bandura, the arousal phase was necessary because otherwise the children in the non-aggressive condition would have no reason to behave aggressively.

13 Whether or not the children had learned aggressive behaviour was measured by observing each child as he or she played for 20 minutes (through a one-way window). The observers used a time sampling observation to record what the child was doing every 5 seconds — they counted imitation of physical aggression, imitative verbal aggression, imitative non-aggressive verbal responses, non-imitative physical and verbal aggression.

14 In Chaney's study the external influence was the whistle that sounded and a spinner/ball that rolled when the inhaler was used correctly. These 'toys' amused the children and provided positive reinforcement to encourage the children to use the inhaler correctly.

15 Qualitative data are rich, detailed, descriptive data.

16 Kohlberg's theory is on the nature side of the debate as his theory of moral development is a maturation theory – changes in moral reasoning are determined by the age of a person and people can only pass through the levels in the age-related order listed.

17 A cross-cultural sample was needed to find out whether the understanding of lying is influenced by cultural norms and moral values because if the understanding of lying is influenced by the cultural norms and moral values in which individuals are raised, then Chinese children who are raised in a collectivist culture may value truth telling or lying differently from Canadian children who are raised in an individualist culture.

18 One advantage of the suggestion that behaviour is caused by nurture is that if this is true then behaviour can be changed. For example, if the culture a child grows up in affects what he or she thinks is 'right or wrong' then exposure to a different culture may change this.

19 The participant stared at a focal point on a screen with one eye covered and images were displayed on the screen — either to the left visual field/right hemisphere or to the right visual field/left hemisphere. To test the language capability of each hemisphere, the participant was asked to describe what was shown on the screen.

20 When a picture was displayed to the left side of the screen and thus to the left visual field processed in the right hemisphere the participant could not describe what was shown or said that nothing was displayed, but when the picture was displayed on the right side of the screen and processed in the left hemisphere they could describe what was shown.

21 There are several differences. Sperry is a snapshot study using experimental methods; Casey is a longitudinal study using correlational analysis. Sperry's participants were 11 adults and Casey's participants were 4-year-old children when the study started. Sperry is a laboratory experiment where the IV is which side of the screen the image was displayed, but Casey is a quasi experiment where each participant is a high delayer or a low delayer. Sperry used inference to decide which side of the brain was active, but Casey used the modern technique of fMRI scanning.

22 When the kittens were born they were put in a dark room. At 2 weeks old, for 5 hours every day, they were put onto a glass table inside a cylinder which was covered with either vertical or horizontal black and white stripes. The kittens wore a collar that restricted their visual field. When the kittens were 5 months old, they were taken out of the cylinder and taken into a well-lit room and were observed to see the impact of this on their behaviour.

23 Brain plasticity means the extent to which the physical structure of the brain can be changed/adapted by environmental factors and/or by behaviour.

24 The aim was to find out whether changes in the brain could be detected in those with extensive navigation experience and London Black Cab taxi drivers have extensive navigation experience, driving daily round thousands of routes around London.

25 There are several differences:
- The Maguire et al. participants are human adult males but Blakemore and Cooper's participants are non-human animals (kittens).
- Maguire et al. breaks no ethical guidelines; Blakemore and Cooper's is unethical.
- Maguire et al. measured brain plasticity looking at pictures of the brain (MRI scans) but Blakemore and Cooper measured changes in the visual system by studying the actual neurons from two cats, one horizontally and one vertically exposed.
- Maguire et al. is a quasi experiment — participants cannot be randomly allocated to be London taxi drivers, but Blakemore and Cooper is a laboratory experiment.

26 Hans developed a phobia of horses, and this phobia was individual to him. The study is a case study of only one participant — Little Hans — and a tremendous amount of detail was gathered about his fears, dreams and fantasies. It is an in-depth study of one child and the cause of his phobia.

27 The data collected are qualitative. One advantage of Hans' father collecting qualitative data is that the result is rich, detailed information that came first hand from Hans about his dreams and fantasies.

28 One reason why this control group was used was because, like Asperger's adults, Tourette's adults have difficulty with social relationships and Baron-Cohen et al. wanted to show that only adults with Asperger syndrome have difficulty reading the emotion shown in eyes.

29 Quantitative data (ordinal level data) were collected in the eyes task.

30 According to Gould, the Army IQ tests measured nurture (not nature) because test scores rose in relation to the number of years an immigrant had lived in the USA (a positive correlation) which suggested that learning rather than innate intelligence was involved.

31 Possible sources of bias:
- The Army IQ tests were only given to men so there is a gender bias in the sample.
- The Army Alpha tests involved writing, yet many of the army recruits were illiterate/uneducated so could not write.
- Many of the army recruits were uneducated so could not read the questions.
- The Army IQ tests were in English, but many of the recruits were recent immigrants who did not understand English.
- Pictures used in the Army Beta test were based on US middle-class culture so could not be understood by the recruits who were recent immigrants.
- Multiple-choice questions were based on US culture so were meaningless to recruits who were recent immigrants.

Index